Becoming American

Becoming American

MY FIRST LEARNING JOURNEY

EDGAR H. SCHEIN

Becoming American

My First Learning Journey

Copyright © 2016 Edgar H. Schein.

iUniverse books may be ordered through booksellers or by contacting:

iUniverse
1663 Liberty Drive
Bloomington, IN 47403
www.iuniverse.com
1-800-Authors (1-800-288-4677)

ISBN: 978-1-4917-8985-8 (sc)
ISBN: 978-1-4917-8986-5 (e)

Print information available on the last page.

iUniverse rev. date: 03/17/2016

Contents

Introduction

This memoir is a series of stories about and reflections on my early life and the launching of my family and my career. These stories help me to understand who I am, what I did, and, most important, what lessons I learned along the way. Good fortune, serendipity, and opportunism played significant roles in how my life evolved, but above all, I have become aware that whatever constraint, danger, or opportunity came my way, I turned it into something that I could benefit from. My first title for these memoirs was *Right Time, Right Place* because I have had the good fortune to live through interesting times and I have had many opportunities handed to me as gifts. But I realized early on the events turned into opportunities only if I could learn from them.

My early experiences taught me to be observant and mindful, and being an only child much praised by my parents, I learned how to learn. So after much dialogue with friends and colleagues, I settled on the subtitle *My Learning Journeys* for the common theme of the several parts of these memoirs because that describes the various pieces of my personal and professional history more accurately.

I am often asked how I came to be an organizational psychologist interested in culture, careers, and the practice of consulting. What role did my early life play in how my interests developed? In this book, I want to reflect on these questions and interweave some of the basic facts of my early life with reflections on how those events influenced me.

1

The basic facts are that I was born in 1928 in Zurich, Switzerland; I lived there for six years; I moved to Odessa in the Soviet Union for three years; I spent one year in Prague; and then I came to Chicago in 1938. I was educated at the University of Chicago, Stanford, and Harvard; spent four postdoctoral years at the Walter Reed Army Institute of Research; and then spent the bulk of my academic years, 1956–2008, at MIT's Sloan School of Management. MIT provided a facilitative climate for what has turned out to be a most satisfying and productive career.

Over those fifty-some years, I have had the unusual experience of being involved in the evolution of five different concepts in the field of organizational psychology— coercive persuasion, career anchors, process consultation, organizational culture, and humble inquiry. In 1965, I wrote one of the first two textbooks on organizational psychology, and I have contributed to the growth of the practice of organization development.

In 1956, I married Mary Lodmell, a wonderful woman who was with me for fifty-two years but who ultimately succumbed to breast cancer at age seventy-six. We had three children, all of whom are married now, who have produced seven grandchildren. We led a rich cultural life of travel, birding, and the opera. I am now eighty-eight, living in a five-star retirement complex in Palo Alto, California, still working and looking back.

Is it possible to write an accurate history about oneself by adhering strictly to the facts—cities and restaurants, universities and jobs, classes taught and books written? I think not, because even one's memory of the facts is highly selective. Some degree of retrospective falsification and memory loss is inevitable, but I have enough clear recollections to tell a series of stories that make collective sense. My early years were punctuated by several major events that I can easily remember and that clearly influenced the path I eventually found myself on.

The emphasis on stories reminds me of an anecdote I heard about Peter Drucker, the eminent management guru. At one of his lectures, he illustrated a point with stories about a company with which he had consulted. During the question-and-answer period, an audience member from this company disputed him: "But, Professor Drucker, what you said about my company did not happen in that way." Allegedly, Drucker reared up and said in his most authoritative manner, "Young man, I tell stories to make a point, not to write history." Hopefully my stories will make some points *and* be historically accurate.

In this book, I want to tell a story about the first part of my life—coming to America, getting educated, and launching my career. In many ways, this is a story of becoming American. The chapters tell the story chronologically, from my early years in Europe to my education in Chicago and at Stanford, Harvard, and the Walter Reed Army Medical Center in Washington, DC. It ends with getting married and setting off on my first job as an assistant professor at MIT's School of Industrial Management. Starting a family and launching a career in Cambridge, Massachusetts, will be covered in the next book.

Chapter 1

Leaving Europe (1928–38)

Zurich (1928–34)

My father, Marcel, was born the younger son of the local banker in the small town of Trstena, Czechoslovakia, in the Tatra Mountains in 1902. As a boy, I met my father's older brother, Nicholas, or "Uncle Mickey"; his beautiful wife, Maja; and my grandmother, but I never met my grandfather. I have no recollection of when he died, and I have never determined how the German-speaking Jewish Schein family ended up in what is today Slovakia, nor how my father ended up being Hungarian in looks and temperament.

When my daughter Louisa and her family visited Trstena in 2002, she could not find any trace of the Schein family, suggesting that during the Hitler era, towns systematically expunged any evidence of Jews living there. The name is clearly German, but both my father and his brother Nicholas had dark complexions and spoke Hungarian fluently.

My father had a bent for science. In order to avoid being drafted into the German Army toward the end of World War I, he was sent off to Heidelberg to learn about physics. In 1925, he went on to pursue a PhD at the University of Zurich, and he established himself there as a Dozent, the equivalent of an assistant professor at the time.

Like so many of his peers in Central Europe, my father learned early on that being Jewish was a problem.

Anti-Semitism was everywhere, resulting in many of his friends in that part of the world converting to Catholicism or, like Marcel, becoming agnostic and trying their best to deny their own Jewishness. While in Zurich at the university, he fell in love with and married Hilde Schoenbeck. It came as no great surprise that he fell for a blonde, blue-eyed Lutheran engineering student from Saxony.

Hilde was the only child of Selma and Max Schoenbeck, a German civil engineer who had spent his career in northern Germany and then retired to Bad Schandau, a resort town on the Elbe in the mountainous part of Saxony that was often called "Little Switzerland." He had been in the German Army and looked resplendent in his Prussian uniform complete with spike-topped helmet in many early photographs. Hilde was sent to the University of Zurich to study engineering, which was most unusual for a woman in those days.

By the time they were married in 1927, Marcel had finished his degree and had taken a job at the University of Zurich. He was well liked by his university mentors and was beginning a comfortable life in Switzerland. Hilde, however, had not finished her degree when they married. I learned many years later that, after they became engaged, Marcel told Hilde, "Go home, and learn to cook. One physicist in the family is enough." And so she did, conforming to what was in those years the proper thing to do. I was born in March of the following year.

By the time I was one and a half, we were already on the move. Marcel and Hilde went off to the University of Chicago, where he got a yearlong fellowship, and I was parked with Grandmother Selma back in Bad Schandau.

The contacts my parents built in Chicago proved to be important for our later emigration. Grandfather Max was still alive, but his Parkinson's disease made him virtually an invalid. Grandmother Selma, on the other hand, was a bundle of energy. I got to know her better in later years and admired the energy she displayed right up to her death at age ninety-five. I don't remember much from this time, but the photos taken of me playing happily on the shore of the Elbe suggest that this period with my grandmother was pleasant, even if being taken away from my parents for a year was, I would assume, somewhat distressing.

Becoming American

When my parents returned, we settled into a comfortable routine in Zurich. We took many trips to the Alps because of my father's hobby of mountain climbing. After climbing in Saxony and Slovakia as a youth, he then ambitiously moved on to the many Swiss peaks. Hilde went along with him on many of his simpler climbs. I inherited their aesthetic appreciation for the mountains but had not the slightest inclination to scale them. Hilde often showed me her broken finger acquired during a rock-climbing expedition with Marcel, serving as a warning not to get interested in this dangerous sport.

My own enchantment with mountains grew from hiking among the spring flowers, which was both physically and aesthetically invigorating. Grassy meadows that drop precipitously into valleys studded with stone-roofed farmhouses and cows that grazed contentedly on hillsides, their bells creating a rural symphony, were imprinted on me. All of this was backdropped by a twelve-thousand-foot massif of snowcapped rock giants seeming to leap raggedly into the sky.

The landscape was defined by its contrasts: the sheer fortress of the Eiger towering over the valley floor separated from the neighboring Jungfrau and Monch by massive glaciers from which mountain streams fed alpine lakes; a colorful riot of wildflowers alongside manicured boxes of geraniums that adorned every balcony and windowsill; the raw gray of the rock face slashed by the shimmering white of the glacier and the snowy upper sides of the peaks that formed the entire horizon. Exposed frequently to such spectacular vistas at a young age, I continue to be stimulated by color and by contrasts, impelled to seek out that which visually arrests.

Zurich itself was a feast for the eyes, with its lake and the surrounding hills and woods. Up one of these hills was the Grand Hotel Dolder, which one reached by means of a funicular. Next to the hotel were tennis courts nestled into the woods, which I still remember because I was asked to play in the clearing next to the courts while my parents played tennis. By age five, I was allowed a few minutes on the court with my own tennis racket, an early start to what was to become my life sport.

Many years later, summering with my wife and three young children in Bryant Pond, Maine, I was reminded of my childhood days in the Swiss mountains. Our cottage looked out across a lake to five-hundred-foot-tall Mount

Christopher, up which we could climb easy trails to view magnificent vistas of the surrounding hills and woods. No huge rock faces here, but I was in heaven nevertheless, feeling comfortable in the woods and on the lake. I was astounded to discover that Mary, who grew up in Carmel—with the California coast's crashing breakers and vast, bright beaches—found the darkness and silence of the woods and lake unsettling, just as I found the Pacific exciting but also unsettling in its raw power.

Mary and I were raised in different families on different continents, and I realized how much our early life experiences determine in what milieus we feel basic comfort. Mary was an ocean person, and I a mountain person. Though she could enjoy wandering the woods to pick berries and mushrooms with me, she preferred combing tidal pools and beaches for unique shells. I could appreciate the coast and came to love it, but I am still struck by how comfortable and stimulated I feel when I am in the woods.

Seeing how deeply a sense of familiarity or security can be tied to early experiences of habitat is eye-opening. Perhaps my childhood home then was not one of the many apartments we rented in various European cities but the stillness of a pine-enshrouded lake—the mountain hulking among the tree gaps, the fragrances of flowers shifting by season. My mother knew mushrooms and taught me how to spot them and how to distinguish the best edible ones from poisonous or ill-tasting ones. To this day, not much can replace the thrill of finding a Pfifferling (chanterelle) or Steinpilz (porcini) in the woods when the season is right.

Back in the city, the life of a spoiled only child included many trips to Café Spruengli for hot chocolate with whipped cream, which had to be consumed in a particular way. The cup of chocolate was heaped with rich and nonaerated whipped cream to be eaten one spoonful at a time, dipped into the chocolate beneath it. An extra dish of whipped cream kept this spooning going until most of the liquid was gone.

Trips downtown also included shopping at Weber, the fabulous toy store. By age six, I had acquired from there a complete Maerklin electric train set, a perfect replica of the real Swiss trains. When I ran it in a darkened room, I loved seeing the cars illuminated by tiny lights inside them and marveled at the perfect reproductions of the real trains that I often traveled in. I also acquired an erector set and a functioning small steam engine, which was quite frightening because it built up enough pressure to drive tiny lathes. The German toys were quite extraordinary in their precision and perfect functioning. Their accuracy of miniaturization captured my imagination and undoubtedly later launched my hobby of collecting netsuke, Japanese miniatures that were used as decorative fobs for tobacco pouches.

Winters were exciting because we all skated on Lake Zurich when it froze over. On holidays, we went into the mountains, where I learned to ski. I especially remember the wonder of Christmas because the tree in our apartment had natural candles clipped onto its branches instead of electric lights. Receiving gifts in candlelight on Christmas Eve was special. This German way of celebrating required me to take a nap in the late afternoon, during which time, I was told, the Christ Child would come by the house and set up presents under the Christmas tree. When I was awakened in the early evening, I was invited to come into the living room, where I would find the lit-up tree on top of a large table. Under the tree sat my train set and other gifts. It was quite spectacular and mysterious.

No one spoke about how the Christ Child managed all this, nor was any rationale given for why the presents came from the Christ Child. When, in later years, I learned about Santa Claus, I also learned that the German equivalent was to celebrate Saint Nicholas Day on December 6 with gifts of candy and marzipan. This celebration had nothing to do with Christmas but laid a greater foundation for my love of marzipan and other fancy candies. Whatever else those early years in Switzerland were, they were rich fare for the eyes and the stomach.

The First Emigration: Odessa or Nanking (1934–36)

Sometime in 1934, Marcel came home with the news that we had to leave Switzerland. He was not sure of the cause, but the Swiss and the Czechs had had a falling out and he, a Czech citizen, would lose his job at the university. I never found out what the conflict was about, but the consequences were severe. Not only would Marcel have to restart his career, but we had to leave the good life in Zurich and our many close friends. Among them was Professor Edgar Meyer, my father's mentor, after whom I was named. At that time, where was a young, ambitious, Jewish experimental cosmic ray physicist to go? Europe was in turmoil, and the United States had not yet launched its programs to provide safe havens for refugee physicists.

There were basically two options for a scientist in the new field of cosmic rays—China and the Soviet Union—because these countries were hungrily building their own science establishments. Marcel had job offers from both Nanking and Odessa. I can only imagine the difficult conversation my parents must have had to decide between these alternatives.

The offer from Odessa stated my father would run a fairly large and prestigious laboratory with access to the Caucasus Mountains, where a high-altitude lab could be set up. Cosmic rays were studied by exposing silver-based photographic plates at high altitudes, where the rays were more frequent and would leave tracks on the silver plates. Scientists then analyzed the tracks to discover new nuclear particles. I think the prospect of having a lab of his own in the mountains appealed to my father, so off we went to Odessa in November 1934. I was six years old.

The Soviet Union tried to impress foreign scientists and treated them like dignitaries. We were given a nice apartment in a new development and privileges at special "Intourist" stores, which were always well stocked with groceries that the locals could not get. My father got a good salary and excellent facilities in which he could pursue his research. He was eager to set up his work on eighteen-thousand-foot-high Mount Elbrus, resulting in many trips to the Caucasus. Incidentally, I learned then that Europe's highest peak was not Mont Blanc in the Alps but Mount Elbrus in the Caucasus.

For me, life in Odessa was not too different from life in Zurich. We had a spacious apartment into which we were able to move most of our good furniture and Oriental rugs acquired in Zurich. We spoke German at home, and instead of being sent to a Russian school, I was individually tutored by German-speaking teachers. We had two cats, Kotlik and Suslik, who would sit on my bed and take care of me if I had a fever. The apartment complex had undeveloped play areas where I quickly developed friendships with a couple of local kids and learned enough Russian to get along easily with them. Unfortunately, I never learned to read or write it. I had brought along all my German toys, including the Maerklin electric train and the steam engine. My friends stood in awe of such toys and spent many hours in our apartment playing with them and learning what life outside the Soviet Union could be.

I learned much from my friends as well. They were clever about what to do outdoors in a newly constructed apartment complex whose grounds had not yet been landscaped. We spent many an hour burning insects with our magnifying glass and catching tarantulas. We caught them by dropping a ball of wax into their holes in the ground, pulling them up, and admiring their big, hairy bodies as they stuck to the wax. We then left them alone to free themselves from the wax and return to their holes.

What stands out for me about these years was, again, the travel, except now our destinations were Crimea, the Caucasus, and the resorts on the Black Sea in Georgia. We would board well-appointed passenger liners for weeklong voyages from Odessa to the ports of Sochi, Sukhumi, and Batumi. We sometimes came across the Crimean Peninsula by car, which involved many hours of driving through extreme desert, followed by a tortuous climb up to the rim of an old crater where, all at once, we would burst into the lushest and most colorful mountainside, which led down to the deep blue of the Black Sea.

The long hikes in the Caucasus revealed alpine dimensions that exceeded those of Switzerland. Instead of quaint valleys and cow-dotted slopes, I found a wilder and more primitive land populated by people in unusual-looking outfits and uniforms. In the Caucasus, my parents often undertook challenging hikes well beyond my capacity. On one such trip, they arranged for a local Cossack to take me on his horse while they hiked from one overnight hut to the next. I was petrified. He wore what I took to be his military uniform and hat, a very colorful ensemble full of ethnic regalia, and as he hoisted me up into his arms, I was convinced that I would never see my parents again. But the ride turned out to be quite exhilarating, and after I was reunited with my parents two hours later, my fear quickly turned into pride and bravado. I couldn't wait to brag to my friends back in Odessa.

On our way to the mountains, we would often go through undeveloped regions. For example, in Svonetsia, people dragged stuff around on sleds because they were not using the wheel for transportation. For years afterward, I made the classic mistake of attributing this to their "primitive culture" until I recently saw films of this area and found that it is both very hilly and very rocky. For all I know, their uneven terrain lent itself better to sleds than wheeled vehicles for hauling heavy items like lumber and rocks.

Deep in the woods of Svonetsia, I had one of the greatest taste experiences of all time—tasting a full glass of wild strawberries bathed in thick local cream. In my later youth, I often wondered whether this undeveloped region was just a fantasy of mine until, many years later, I met a fellow member of the Harvard Travellers Club who had traveled through the same region and confirmed that Svonetsia really existed and it wasn't merely the manufactured memory of an eight-year-old who loved wild strawberries and caviar.

The caviar story resulted from our ship travel on the Black Sea. On these voyages, the ship's dining rooms often had good caviar available, and it became family gossip how amused and generous the waiters were when they learned how much caviar a scrawny eight-year-old could put away. I rapidly got a reputation for being a young gourmand. On one of these trips, local inefficiency led to an especially epicurean time. We were in Sukhumi on a holiday, awaiting the departure of our regular Black Sea liner. The Soviets had orchestrated a special scientific congress for Sukhumi and planned to flaunt their success by chartering a small luxury liner, no doubt leftover from czarist days, and stock it with all the very best in food and wine.

Just before the end of the congress, it was discovered that the smaller ship could not accommodate all the participants, so at the last minute, the congress members were switched to the bigger Black Sea liner we were booked on. There was no time to switch cargo, so we tourists were sent to the small ship with all the luxuries still on board. The caviar flowed, and the first-class cabin was unforgettable. I adjusted to that lifestyle just fine.

All these pleasures began to fade by mid-1937 as Stalin began his purges. We knew, of course, that such purges were going on, but they only hit us personally when we discovered one morning that a family we were friendly with in our apartment building had suddenly disappeared without a trace or an explanation. I think my father's fear of being both Jewish and a foreigner then kicked in strongly. He resurrected his contacts with the University of Chicago, and the difficult emigration process became a reality. We could not stay in Odessa, but fortunately, my father had acquired a temporary job in Prague.

And so we packed up again. The immediate cost of this decision was we had to leave most of our good furniture, rugs, and clothing behind due to severe restrictions on what one could take out of the Soviet Union. We were allowed only one full shipping container. I had to abandon most of my good toys, which, at age nine, was traumatic. My toys were my only keepsakes from the good years in Zurich, and they had been, in my eyes, essential to making friends in Odessa. To compensate for my loss, I was promised a Schwinn bicycle if and when we got to the United States. How I knew about Schwinn bicycles, I have no idea, but at the time, it seemed like reasonable compensation for the loss of my precious Maerklin trains.

Waiting Places: Prague and Zurich (1937–38)

I knew very little about the negotiations that my father was conducting with various universities, but the position in Prague provided a temporary safe haven. We moved into an apartment, and I was enrolled in a German-speaking elementary school for the year. This was a significant time for me because I was sent to a school that provided a rigorous education but also taught me how much I do not like regimentation. We had to sit very straight, often with our hands behind our backs, while listening to very formal and rigid instruction. I learned a lot, got good grades, and benefited greatly from learning excellent penmanship, but mostly I remember hating it because of the formal behavior that it required.

It was in Prague that I first encountered American culture. We had a movie theater that sometimes screened cartoons between features. The most memorable of these was *Popeye the Sailor Man*. To illustrate how powerful such experiences can be, I can still see clearly in my mind's eye Popeye's exasperation when he had to take action to save Olive Oyl—how he would swallow a whole can of spinach and instantly have enormous muscles with which to destroy evil and save the girl. I had never seen cartoons before, so it is perhaps not surprising that this image was so powerful.

During the Prague year, it became apparent to my father that with Hitler's rise, it was no longer safe to remain in Czechoslovakia. Fortunately, he had begun planning for emigration when he and my mother had visited the University of Chicago in 1930, and now, in 1938, he was able to secure an appointment as an instructor in the Physics Department of the university where Arthur Compton, with the help of the Rockefeller Foundation, was bringing over many physicists, including Enrico Fermi and Leo Szilard. While Marcel made arrangements, he asked my mother and me to move to Zurich to be safe.

I finished my year in school, and in May 1938, we returned to Zurich, where we were to wait until we got word from Marcel in Chicago that it was time to come over. During that time, my mother and I also visited Oma Selma, my grandmother, in Bad Schandau, leaving me with the unfortunate memory of my grandfather with severe Parkinson's disease. This would be our last visit until many years after the war was over.

Needless to say, all of this required a good deal of money, which my parents did not have, so they borrowed from friends and relatives. Marcel's parents could not provide support. His mother had died while we were in Odessa, but his older brother, Nicholas, who immigrated to South America and become a fairly successful businessman in Bolivia and Argentina, did lend us some money. Without his help and that of several close colleagues, our emigration would not have been feasible. This pattern for getting out of Europe was fairly common, later resulting in many lean years in the United States while debts were being paid off.

Life in Zurich in early 1938 was again a lark. I was ten years old, now able to appreciate all the more the beauty of the city and its food. My fancy tastes did not fade but turned from caviar to *schlag* (whipped cream) and mayonnaise. I still remember the food court in one of the major department stores, Jelmoli, where there were endless interesting egg, sausage, and vegetable salads made with mayonnaise. But the ultimate treat was again Café Spruengli, where the pastries and cakes were outdone by hot chocolate with large quantities of schlag.

The downside of this life was, of course, the uncertainty of when and under what circumstances we would get the message to come to Chicago. While I was living it up, my mother had to uphold our morale while we waited and worried. For me, Café Spruengli was the daily highlight; for my mother, it was probably a tactic to keep our spirits up while our future was very much up in the air. Our friends in Zurich regaled us with horrifying stories of how unsafe Chicago would be based on newspaper accounts of the escapades of Al Capone and various other Chicago gangsters.

The telegram and subsequently the tickets for ship travel to the United States arrived in the fall of 1938. We were to take a train to LeHavre, get on a ship there to take us to New York, and then take another train to Chicago. In the compartment of our train to LeHavre, we met a Mrs. Rothman and her two sons, Frank and Steve. They were from Budapest and in the same situation as my mother and I in that Dr. Rothman, a dermatologist, had also gone ahead to make arrangements in the United States. Coincidentally, they were also going to the University of Chicago because Dr. Rothman had secured a position in the medical school. The Rothmans, in contrast to Marcel, had converted to Catholicism, which later struck me as strange since they looked more Jewish than we did and they had not changed their name.

Steve was my age; we became friends quickly. On board the ship, Steve, his little brother Frank, and I played happily together while my mother and Mrs. Rothman struggled with a bit of mal de mer. I learned when they had recovered that our racing around and being pranksters or a nuisance had "terrorized" the ship. Of course, I conveniently have no memory of what we actually did, but we bragged endlessly about the fact that we did not get seasick while our wimpy mothers did.

Arrival in Chicago (October 1938)

My father had been given an instructorship in the Physics Department of the University of Chicago. Though he had by then twelve years of research experience, the US system required one to start at the bottom to prove one's worth, and only then could one rise fast. He was a talented experimental physicist; he had already done important work in the field of cosmic rays and particle physics in the Soviet Union, and he was set to build a similar program of research in Chicago.

Marcel's talent proved itself, so he achieved full professorship status within a few years. He continued high-altitude research by sending stacks of silver emulsion plates into the stratosphere by means of a string of balloons. When the balloons lost lifting power, the stack descended into some field in the Midwest where graduate students recovered it and brought it back for analysis of the tracks that the cosmic rays had left when they encountered and split atoms.

Being deeply in debt meant frugal living. We had a small apartment in Hyde Park and a tight food budget. None of this mattered much to me because I had had enough caviar and pastries and found equivalent delight in canned fruit salad, which was occasionally served as a special treat. This led to occasional upset when fruit salad was bought for guests' dessert and I did not even get to pick the one or two cherries in each can. Later on, I discovered the Tropical Hut, which roasted chicken and ribs on a vertical grill and produced arguably the best ribs I've ever had.

While food clearly remained a focus of our well-being, my attention shifted to learning the language and attending an American school. I had had no English instruction anywhere in previous years, so I hit Chicago with no biases or accent even though or maybe because of the fact that I had learned Russian and Czech. Learning these other languages probably made the task of learning English a lot easier.

At home, we continued to speak German although Marcel and Hilde had learned English, which they spoke with a pronounced accent. My friends Steve and Frank Rothman spoke some English, so they adapted immediately but never overcame their accents. As we settled into life in Chicago, our Americanization began in earnest with the decision to send me to the local public school. True to their promise, my parents bought me a Schwinn bicycle. I was ten years old and ready.

Chapter 2
Growing Up in Chicago
(1938–45)

Ray School, Language Learning, and "Penner"

My first memory of school in America was one of humiliation. Because I didn't know English, Ray School put me back *two* grades. They thought it best that I acclimate in a less-demanding environment, never considering what it felt like to be demoted after getting such good grades in Prague. Fortunately, I was used to picking up languages by now, so I learned fast and was placed back in my appropriate fifth-grade class after only one semester. Little did I know that the real work of acculturation was done outside of and literally on the school walls.

Sports had not been a big part of my life up to that point. I had played a bit of soccer and dabbled in tennis and skiing but had no real hand–eye coordination because no sports had required it—until now. American sports were all about use of the hands. The side of the school building had a ledge about one foot above the ground. If one threw a tennis ball against its sharp edge, the ball would bounce back with great force. Teams were made up of two batters who took turns hitting the ball against the ledge and two people in the field who stood back to catch the ball—one person about five feet away, the infielder, and one person who stood back about twenty feet, the outfielder.

If the ball was caught before touching the ground, it was an out. If it was not caught, depending on how far it went before it touched the ground, it was a single, double, triple, or home run if it went over the outfielder's head. It was scored like baseball, with each pair getting three outs and then changing positions between batting and fielding. This game, called penner, was played by endless numbers of two-person teams all along the edge of that side of the school wall.

Skill was needed in batting to hit the crack at just the right angle and with great force; skill was needed in fielding, especially by the front person because the ball could come at him with such great velocity. Reputations were made, and scores were remembered. I knew the stakes for getting into the game were high, and I was terrified but determined because the sport did not need language skills. As it turned out, I had excellent hand–eye coordination. Penner was my first real taste of American youth culture, and more important, it gave me a foothold in schoolyard society.

On the other side of the school, there was a regular baseball diamond for Chicago-style softball. This was played with a twelve-inch ball that became very soft very fast, allowing us to play on a smaller field without gloves. Pitching was done underhand, so hitting the ball was easy, but hitting it past people on the small field was not because the ball was so soft that it always flew slowly. You could catch fly balls easily, and grounders were usually picked up and successfully thrown to first for the out. Home runs over the fence only occurred early in a game when a new ball that had not yet become soft was brought out.

I learned quickly that penner was for the younger and smaller kids. Anyone could play it, and there was room for many teams along the wall. Softball on the diamond was for the older kids after school, and you had to earn your way into that game with demonstrated skill. I became a pretty good first baseman and a fairly decent hitter, which meant that the guys who mattered eventually accepted me.

Learning the rudiments of the language—vocabulary and grammar—came easily to me because I had a good ear and a flexible tongue from previous language learning. When and how to use the language was a bit more complicated, as I learned the hard way. Trying to keep up with the routine good-humored taunting, I called one of my schoolmates a son of a bitch. He replied by hitting me squarely on the chin and growling, "Don't you ever insult my mother." I had obviously not learned under what conditions it was okay to use this phrase—a phrase I had heard used many times by others. It forcefully reminded me how important it is to be cautious and observant when entering a new culture or situation. I had failed to understand not only *what* can be said but *when* it can be said.

Beyond the sports scene, the years at the Ray School are a blur. I did well in school, but all I remember are penner and softball and the friendships I made surrounding the games. The classes were forgettable. It was, of course, more important to learn the elements of US culture than the three Rs. I learned American English very rapidly, never developed an accent, and could easily lose my European self in the schoolyard. My parents had a much harder time with English and US ways, so I often had to explain to them how many things worked. My grasp of the culture gave me a lot of power and autonomy at home, and I often exploited this freedom to spend most of my time after school with my buddies.

Hyde Park High and the "Syndicate"

We were living in a university neighborhood amid other faculty families. The University of Chicago had a well-known "Lab School," which faculty brats could attend for free, so a difficult decision on where to go to high school had to be made in 1941. Everyone knew that kids who went to the Lab School were namby-pambies, and we were all aware of other faculty kids who never considered anything but public school. I think my parents would have been happy to have me go to the Lab School, but my friends and I decided that it was out of the question. Hyde Park High it was.

Hyde Park High was a huge school occupying an entire square block and housing more than three thousand students. It was only a half mile from my house, but to get to it, one had to cross the Midway, a block-long stretch of grass leftover from the great turn-of-the-century exposition. In the winter, the grassy depressions of the Midway flooded and froze for skating. The Midway was also a nightmarish wind tunnel. I still have frostbitten ears from the frigid winter crossings.

In school, we sorted ourselves very quickly by the kinds of classes we took and by the degree to which we identified with the intellectual crowd versus the athletes or just plain jocks. We were also acutely aware of the social-class stratification among a large contingent of black kids, lower-class white kids, and the rest of us middle-class types. Nowhere was this more apparent than where we hung out during recess and lunch. My buddies and I were the intellectual elite, a kind of elite that isn't necessarily at the top of the status ladder in a public high school. We hung around in an area at the back of the building where we felt safe though isolated.

Of our classes, I remember best the math courses I took with the legendary Beulah Shoesmith. She perfectly fit the stereotype of the spinsterish, uncompromising classroom martinet and threw small pieces of chalk with deadly accuracy at the foreheads of students who did not pay proper attention. We not only learned what was required but, beyond this, acquired real respect for the wonders of the intellectual realms that mathematics opened up. In later years, when our careers had jelled, we discovered how many of Ms. Shoesmith's students went into science and other academic fields.

We also enjoyed our chemistry and shop classes, which enabled us to turn our academic interests and talents to somewhat more questionable activities. There were five of us, and like any clique worth its salt, we had a name that conveyed the appropriate combination of swagger and mystery: the Syndicate. Bradford Lytle, the son of a professor of divinity and a well-known local pacifist, had in his family's house a well-equipped basement with a lathe, a drill press, and various other tools. Thus, the Syndicate had everything we needed to apply our imaginations and intellectual talents to various "challenging" projects.

We experimented a lot, and one of our achievements was constructing a BB gun with which we could shoot squirrels. But our most ambitious undertaking was to sink the *Nina*, the full-scale replica of one of Columbus's ships that was anchored in a lagoon in Jackson Park. To make it suitably challenging and dramatic, we designed a torpedo by soldering a platform onto two tennis-ball cans and then added two warheads filled with gunpowder made from various chemicals available in drugstores. On top of the platform, we constructed a battery-driven motor that moved a propeller. Next to the motor was a timer linked to a detonator that would explode the warheads at a certain time based on our calculation of how long it would take the torpedo to cross the lagoon and arrive at the *Nina*'s side.

Needless to say, this took much planning and many months of gathering materials; constructing the motor, the timer, and the torpedo; mixing various chemicals to make our gunpowder; and loading the gunpowder carefully into the specially constructed front ends of the tennis-ball cans. When we finally finished it, we went to the lagoon early one morning, set the timer, and launched our torpedo. Its distance to the ship was about a third of a mile, so we watched with great anticipation as our torpedo made its way slowly across the lagoon. It was almost out of sight when it approached the ship's side, but our timer had been accurate, and the explosion was imminent. We waited and waited, but the only thing that happened was that our torpedo sank. We never determined what had gone wrong. Though we never admitted it to ourselves, we all breathed a collective sigh of relief that this gross act of vandalism had failed.

As I think about this teenage prank, what strikes me is the elaborateness of it and the amount of knowledge, skill, and patience it took to execute it. But we were not nerds. In fact, we spent much more time on sports and card games than on reading and studying.

Softball and penner disappeared for us in high school, but touch football on the Midway became a major preoccupation when the weather was good. I was nimble and tall, so I enjoyed being an end. We did not block in touch football, so agility and dodging were the main skills needed.

I loved running and catching passes. One year, a newcomer entered our game. He lined up on defense opposite, and when the ball was snapped, he jumped forward, grabbed me by the shoulders, and threw me to the ground, hard. I could hardly believe it. I reeled from so much contact, but his authoritative announcement that in touch football it was okay to block even if there was no tackling quickly invalidated my outrage. This was a new rule to all of us, and an especially painful bit of learning for me since I had become the key exemplar. I felt unfairly treated by this physical assault and, because I had no inclination to block or tackle others, found myself avoiding games in which this person was playing. But I learned the important lesson that rules vary by who announces and chooses to enforce them. I have never liked contact sports, and I continue to avoid physical confrontation.

Hockey and figure skating took over in the winter when the grassy depression flooded to create good ice skating. In our hockey play, we made it a point *not* to run into each other. We played on the Midway when there was free ice available and in the rink under Stagg Field at other times. My parents were avid figure skaters themselves; they had taught me the art and equipped me with excellent figure skates. Like everyone, I aspired to do figure eights, forward and backward, waltz turns, even small jump turns. Skating gracefully to piped-in music was not only good exercise but very romantic.

In our high school, amateurish, noncontact hockey, I could hold my own. My figure skates, with their broader blades and sharper edges, gave me an advantage in our little scrub games where agility was more important than speed.

We all thought we were pretty good and thoroughly enjoyed our games until the arrival one winter of a young Canadian man with the skill called stick handling, as yet unbeknownst to us. Not only was he a better skater than the rest of us, but he would also challenge any three or four of us to stop him if he tried to take the puck past us. By lifting our stick at the right moment, batting our stick away, and dodging around us, he could do just what he had announced—go through us like a hot knife through butter. It was both humiliating and awesome to watch him stop, start, and circle around us without touching anything but our sticks.

When we could not play outdoors, we played cards, Ping-Pong, and Monopoly. Hearts, bridge, and poker were our favorite card games. We especially loved hearts because of the possibility of "shooting the moon" and the pleasure we all got out of dumping the queen of spades on an unsuspecting fellow player. I realized in later years how much these days taught me about card sense and game playing. As an only child, I had a lot to learn about how to handle feelings of competition, how to win, and, more important, how to lose. The tension of gambling, especially in poker, is still with me because winning and losing are not so much a matter of money gain or loss but a test of one's own judgment and decision making. To this day, I do not like the feeling of having made a bad judgment on a poker hand, and I therefore tend to avoid games where I cannot figure out what the judgment factor is.

As I observe what my grandchildren do these days after school, I am awed by how much has changed in sixty or so years. We had lots of free time; kids today have hardly any. I wonder what different things they are learning compared to what I learned when not in the classroom. One important thing I have learned is not to judge the world they live in. I have no sympathy for those of my peers who lament what the kids of today do or don't do. My admonition to myself and to my judgmental peers is "Don't judge them; watch them, and learn from them."

Tennis: Play and Work

Tennis was my parents' sport, but except for the days in Zurich on Dolder Hill, it had not been part of their lives. In Odessa and Prague, they had a few opportunities, but it was always taken for granted that it was our sport. This changed dramatically when we discovered that the University of Chicago's Quadrangle Club, the school's faculty club, boasted three well-maintained clay tennis courts open to faculty and their families. My parents had regular matches there and took me onto the court frequently so my mother could teach me the basic strokes.

I took to it immediately. Though I never had any formal lessons, by the time I was in high school, I was good enough to try out for the team, and by my senior year, I was the number-two singles player on the squad. Hyde Park High was in a city league, so we got to visit other high schools in the region, play on some unbelievably bad asphalt courts, and earn the respect of fellow students who could not make a team. My high school letter for tennis is one of my most prized achievements.

Playing with my parents and watching them play taught me a lot about them and about sports etiquette. My mother had talent and played a solid game. My father was full of enthusiasm and played very intensely but had less skill, so he would often miss shots and display a surprising amount of petulance. I think my mother always let him win. When I got good enough to beat him, we stopped playing each other. In chess as well as in tennis, my father did not like to lose to his growing son and would have minor temper tantrums when he was not winning.

Tennis is a lonely sport in that there is really no one to blame when things go badly. I remember well how missing an easy shot could produce the impulse to smash a tennis racket against something and in other ways display the rage that is born of frustration. Sometimes, after missing a shot, I would stare at my racket as if *it* had missed the shot, or I would look at the offending mound of clay that had caused the bad bounce that accounted for my miss. Winning and losing in tennis were great teachers of how to handle elation and frustration in that you eventually realize that you are out there on the court entirely on your own and that whatever happens is your own doing. As I got better and could beat my father, I lost respect for him if he pouted and complained. If he insisted on playing, I usually let him win by deliberately missing my shots.

I learned later that I could feel very different when playing with my son. We taught him tennis early. He became a very good player and also exhibited temper tantrums when not playing up to his standard, but when he got good enough to beat me, I found this exciting and could admire his shots and encourage him. I often found myself rooting for him when we were evenly matched.

The Quadrangle Club became a significant factor in my high school life because it provided my first work opportunity. I answered the club's phone. The phone system was old and required you to plug the wire of the incoming call into the appropriate hole for where the call had to go, so an operator needed to manage it. The switchboard was right at the front desk, which was also the place to sign up for courts, sell cigarettes, make dinner reservations, and deal with other questions related to club matters. During my high school years, I worked for several hours a week on the switchboard and managed the front desk, which, for a teenager, was a lot of responsibility and provided a decent income.

The best part of the job was that I got to meet many famous professors who were guests at the club. I also noted how professors from different fields got to know and respect each other through joint activities, such as tennis, bridge, and billiards. It was a tribute to this faculty club that so many cross-disciplinary friendships were made from providing professors opportunities to play together. One of the regular doubles games included professors of Sanskrit, chemistry, theology, and psychology. I would marvel at the extended locker-room conversations that I overheard, and I always regretted that MIT had not created a club in which such interdisciplinary conversations could occur.

The club had a number of guest rooms for visitors and allowed a couple of professors to live there permanently. I loved the opportunity to secretly visit one of these apartments, where a professor of Oriental studies had an incredible collection of mysterious objects, most of which I could not identify but could admire. This professor had, at that time, what we would have described as "effeminate" gestures—a self-presentation that today is clearly characteristic of some gay men.

My friends and I knew, of course, that homosexuality existed and was viewed negatively by everyone. We had also learned that there was such a thing as latent homosexuality, which was a source of great anxiety because it might reflect our true self. However, one could not talk openly about this in the 1940s. One suffered silently with one's fears and self-doubts. I viewed this professor as an amusing and harmless eccentric but loved looking at his memorabilia.

Viewing such objects often triggered a fantasy, which always filled me with longing based on what I avidly read in *The Arabian Nights* in German when I was ten. I learned in these stories that the young prince usually had free run of the palace, but there was always one door to a room that he was never to enter. He did enter it, of course, and he found himself in a magnificent garden. While admiring it, he saw a huge flock of birds descend to the central pool. Then he saw them shed their feathers and turn into a group of drop-dead beautiful women surrounding a princess, with whom he immediately fell hopelessly in love. She pledged herself to him but had to return to her homeland, where he would have to find her. The rest of the story described his incredible adventures in seeking her out. I always assumed that this homeland would have been somewhere in the Orient and that the stories reflected the degree to which Arab traders found their way to China and Japan over the centuries.

This sense of longing for something discovered but unavailable has always stayed with me. Even later visits to Japan and China did little to change this feeling, but I did develop a love of Japanese netsuke and still regard "the Orient" as mysterious and inscrutable. When my oldest daughter became an anthropologist with an emphasis on Chinese minority groups, she often reminded me that "the Orient" was no longer a politically correct concept and that the term *Orientalism* was a product of nineteenth-century British society. But I loved my fantasy and poking about in this professor's apartment.

Famous Physics Professors at Home

The University of Chicago became a hothouse of physics in part due to the efforts of Arthur Compton, who throughout the early Hitler years had made it a project to recruit European professors and financially help them immigrate to the United States. With the help of foundations, he had assembled an incredible collection of physicist émigrés from all parts of Europe who then were scattered among various universities, such as MIT, Columbia, Cornell, Princeton, the University of California at Berkeley, Cal Tech, and especially the University of Chicago. Many of these physicists began to work on creating a chain reaction and later were instrumental in the creation of the atom bomb. My father knew most of them and frequently had them over for various parties.

To me, they were merely party guests. People like Enrico Fermi, Leo Szilard, and their students and colleagues seemed to be a crowd of head-in-the-sky nerds, able to debate intellectual matters well past midnight. But they were also very down-to-earth and enthusiastic about ordinary social and athletic activities like camping, hiking, and mountain climbing. They were fun loving, they never took themselves too seriously, they were very informal, and they certainly did not let on that the work they were doing was monumentally significant for the future of the world.

Fermi, for example, was a restless spirit who, instead of sitting like everyone else, would just wander around aimlessly, looking at everything and having bits of conversation here and there. My most striking memory of him is based on an encounter that occurred years after I finished my PhD. I proudly brought home a three-hundred-page dissertation describing my experiments on imitation. My father insisted that we leave it on the coffee table so that guests would see it.

At one evening party while I was visiting home, I observed Fermi pick up the thesis and go into a corner of the living room to leaf through it. After ten minutes, he beckoned me over to him and proceeded to ask a series of questions about the experiment and its significance. It astonished me that these were better and tougher questions than my colleagues or thesis committee had asked me. In just ten minutes of browsing, he got to the deepest and most controversial issues in my research!

Szilard, on the other hand, was an urbane, well-spoken Hungarian intellectual in the best sense. He had a tremendous sense of humor and would effortlessly entertain everyone with sophisticated jokes and stories. His intellect was not as visible as Fermi's except in the quality of his anecdotes. Szilard was a masterful storyteller, able to bring together all the eccentric types assembled in our living room. It shouldn't have surprised me when I learned years later how essential he had been in convincing the president and others in our government to pursue development of the nuclear bomb.

As the threat of war grew in the early 1940s, conversations at home became more serious around the need for and a fear of a nuclear chain reaction that could become the basis of a weapon. My father stuck to experimenting with the study of cosmic rays, but Szilard and Einstein convinced President Roosevelt to push nuclear research, resulting in

Fermi successfully producing a chain reaction under the stands of Stagg Field in 1942. It dawned on me that the men I dutifully handed cocktails to were irreversibly changing the field of atomic physics and the world.

Even as physicists all over the country began to mobilize around the Manhattan Project and went to Los Alamos to actually build the bomb, my father remained firmly committed to the experimental study of cosmic rays. He devoted himself entirely to his own experimental procedures of sending silver emulsions forty thousand feet or more above the earth by means of a chain of balloons. The most exciting part of this for me in my early teens was going to Stagg Field, the old football stadium where the chain reaction occurred, and watch some twenty or thirty fifteen-foot balloons being inflated and tied together until they had enough lift to take the heavy box of silver plates up into the stratosphere.

When the balloons gradually lost their lift, the box of equipment would gradually float down and land in some farmer's field a hundred miles away. Whoever found the equipment was to call the university, give their location, and await the graduate student crew, who drove out to reclaim the equipment as quickly as possible. Then they would analyze the data of the tracks, which the cosmic rays had made on the silver plates.

This research was fundamental particle physics and was highly regarded. My father was an important member of the community that was studying these matters in cyclotrons and other "atom smashers" to create tracks similar to what my father's silver emulsions showed, all in the search for new particles. He had become a full professor in 1946, just eight years after arriving as an instructor.

With my father's career going well, our debts were gradually paid off, and we moved to a bigger apartment in which I could not only have a room of my own but also install a big desk and bookcase. I remember well how important it was to me to have a room in which I could organize my books and possessions to my own liking. I also had a radio and always played classical music whenever I was in the room. It made studying easier because it dampened the sounds of my parents talking or arguing.

They usually argued about work issues in the surprisingly cutthroat world of experimental physics. As I learned from listening to my father, there was fierce competition among the experimental physicists as to who would publish findings first. Marcel's unofficial rival was Bruno Rossi at MIT, who was also studying new particles but used a cyclotron to bombard atoms in order to create the data. The hunt for new particles was a kind of gold rush, as physicists believed that the discoveries were not only fundamental but also the key to Nobel Prizes.

Every year, there was great speculation about who would be nominated, who deserved it, and who did *not* deserve it and consternation about the unfairness of who got it. I will never know whether people were actually stealing each other's work or failing to acknowledge each other, but there were many emotional evenings when Marcel would engage in borderline paranoid rants that both my mother and I had to deal with. That usually meant listening and providing counterarguments and a great deal of reassurance. I found myself getting upset and withdrawing to my room to listen to classical music as soon as possible. I was interested in the world of science but not the professional politics.

As I was becoming more Americanized and also a teenager, the distance between my parents and me grew. I became impatient with their lack of understanding of how the United States worked, and I looked forward to getting out on my own at the University of Chicago.

Acculturation and Religion

The most significant thing about my acculturation experiences is how few of them I remember specifically. The incidents I've described stand out as major events in a stream of very vague half memories and images. It is as if the process of adapting, observing carefully, trying to figure things out, and learning the language were sufficiently demanding to block out a lot of what went on. I was very aware of needing to be successful and accomplishing whatever challenges I encountered.

I was also acutely aware of comparing myself to Steve Rothman, the boy I met coming over on the ship. He was not as agile as I, so he was less skilled in sports. He had a strong accent, so he was not as adept with the language, but he had a little brother with whom to play, so he was not as alone. Relative to Steve, I was winning the Americanization game through the powerful socialization role of sports, and that seemed the most important then. I began to take my Americanization for granted in that not having an accent made it easy for me to "pass." When people found out I had immigrated at age ten, they were always surprised. I later learned that if one wants to learn Standard American English, Chicago is the place to do it. Chicago English is radio-announcer English.

But language was only one part of passing. My father's explicit rejection of Jewishness in particular and religion in general became very clear to me as we settled into our first

Chicago apartment in 1938, and the decision was made to have me confirmed as a Lutheran. The Rothmans, along with many other Hungarian Jews, had become practicing Catholics, but my agnostic father had married blonde, blue-eyed Hilde, who had been confirmed as a Lutheran in her childhood. She was essentially indifferent to religion, however, and I do not remember ever going to church, even on holidays. If there was a formal event, we went to the Rockefeller Chapel at the University of Chicago, but these events were always nondenominational. Nevertheless, I was to be confirmed as a Lutheran, so I had to go to the dreaded class and learn all the essentials. My becoming officially Lutheran was simply a tactic to avoid being half-Jewish, as I saw it, and to pass completely, as my father saw it.

I remember well my father's ranting about the prevalence of anti-Semitism and how important it would be for no one to know I was half-Jewish. I remember being forced to go to the confirmation classes, being bored, being confirmed, and feeling nothing. At some point, it was proposed that I change my name to Shayne, a good Irish name, and with my blond hair, I could abandon this dangerous identity—my clandestine half-Jewishness. In retrospect, it was all a charade that accomplished little more than to confuse me forever. Even if I could pass, I clearly felt tainted and vulnerable. Changing my name seemed absurd in the end, so the main goal then became to forget about religion. But, of course, one can't.

To this day, I am sensitive when it comes to my religious heritage because I picked up some of the anti-Semitism. In a certain sense, I wanted nothing to do with Jewishness, and I came to dislike what I later identified as the New York Jew stereotype: the loud, domineering, fast-talking

Jew who intimidated me. I did not like people who were verbally aggressive in this way, and I dreaded the thought that I might well be perceived the same way.

This mild anti-Semitism showed up in my later life in that neither my wife, Mary, nor I ever had much interest in visiting Israel, and both of us expressed a dislike of the loud and aggressive Jew. Mary's father was somewhat anti-Semitic, and I've never known whether he fully approved of me. He and Mary's mother were of Scandinavian origin—Norwegian and Finnish—so my arriving with my Jewish name might have caused a bit of dismay; I was always a bit sensitive around them as a result.

Mary had been raised in the congregational church, so when we arrived in Cambridge in 1956, we sought out the local church and joined it. We enjoyed the social side and went to church on some Sundays but, after a year or so, dropped out because it made new demands on us to which we could not accede. Specifically, Mary was asked to be on a variety of committees, and I was asked to help teach Sunday school. By this time, we had a child and did not feel that we had either the time or the commitment to get involved more deeply with the church.

I find myself assessing these feelings frequently in that, even though I consider myself quite indifferent to the whole issue, I am overcome with irritation when I receive yet another e-mail from MIT Hillel or the Joint Jewish Charities when I have told them over and over again that I am not a practicing Jew. Yet I know that I am vulnerable to this mysterious force, this anti-Semitism, which I inherited from my father to some degree, and that it is embedded in my identity with both known and unknown effects.

Chapter 3
The University of Chicago
(1945–47)

I took going to the University of Chicago after Hyde Park High for granted. I don't recall any consideration of alternatives, fretting about getting in, or financial issues. I assume that as a faculty child, I was able to attend without heavy tuition fees, but we never discussed the issue. At that time, the school still used the Great Books program that Hutchins had instituted—a broad two-year general education program that would lead to a bachelor's degree and prepare you to go directly into a master's degree program.

The design was four main courses followed by three-hour multiple-choice tests at the end of each semester. Each course had an extensive reading list, weekly lectures, and optional section meetings. The reading list was published at the beginning of the semester so it was possible to miss lectures and sections and still be able to pass the final exam. Most of us attended lectures if the lecturer was captivating. Few of us went to sections except for humanities courses in which the discussion was interesting.

In the first year, the courses were basic general education in history, philosophy, science, economics, and the arts. We read Plato, Aristotle, Rousseau, Hume, Darwin, and other foundational thinkers. The emphasis was on appreciating depth of knowledge and learning how to think.

In the second year, we continued to take foundational courses but had room for various electives as well. Among these was a course that became a conversation piece for the rest of our lives—OII, pronounced "Oh Eye Eye," or "Observation, Interpretation, and Integration." In this class, we would take a basic reading, such as a chapter out of Plato, and analyze all of its various themes and elements in great detail. Or we would deconstruct a poem, such as "Ode on a Grecian Urn," down to a word-by-word analysis. The point was to get us to understand how carefully crafted much of classical knowledge is and to build respect for the wisdom of the ages while sharpening our analytical skills. We all joked about it and pretended not to care yet learned an enormous amount and did learn to think.

Socialization of an Only Child: Life in Delta Upsilon

I was dying to get out of my parents' apartment, so when I was invited into the Delta Upsilon fraternity in the spring of 1946, I jumped at the chance. I moved into a triple room with one other pledge and one older senior. For the first time, I experienced how different life is when you are not an only child. I had a lot of adjusting to do, especially when it came to all the ribbing and teasing from older and less intellectual brothers. My athletic skills once again saved me from being stereotyped as just a nerd, so I hung out with the more regular guys. We played a lot of Ping-Pong, poker, and bridge; drank a lot; and sometimes watched a terrible black-and-white version of a stag movie with great anticipation and tension. I gladly soaked up the fraternal life.

We went through the usual hazing inside the fraternity house, but I do not remember it ever being humiliating. The end of hell week involved groups of two of us being blindfolded and driven into the woods late at night without food, money, or flashlights and being left there. The object was to give us a mini-survival experience and "test our manhood." We stumbled around, found our way to a road, flagged down a car, hitchhiked back to a familiar neighborhood, and then either walked or hitched back to campus, feeling extremely self-satisfied. This mini-version of the famed aboriginal walkabout—sending adolescents into the wild to learn how to survive and thereby become real men—was appreciated. It tested us and gave us an adventure, but at no time did it humiliate or endanger us.

My tennis skills were not good enough for me to make the regular university team, but I was the number-seven person on the squad, which made me the first substitute at interschool competitions, and this made me feel very proud. Unfortunately, I never was needed, so I didn't experience the agony and the ecstasy of college-level competition.

One of the stars on the team, Bill Tully, was a fellow DU known not only for his tennis but for his life philosophy: "What did you expect? Intelligence?" This cynical phrase became the bedrock of our view of daily events and was used every time any sort of problem, issue, or behavioral fault was discussed. Tully was a senior when I was a freshman, so he played up the wise-man role and taught us all how futile it was to expect anything intelligent from others or, indeed, from life in general. Did Tully turn us all into cynics? Not really, because his overuse of this answer to everything made us realize that he did not really believe it. But it was a convenient way to avoid having to really get into an issue.

As I look back on this period, it strikes me that in all our contemporary commentary on the pathologies of fraternity life—excessive drinking, hazing, and juvenile partying— we fail to appreciate the important process of socialization of the younger members by the older members. I really learned how to get along with others from talks and advice doled out from older brothers. The senior in our triple room was Don Anderson from Enid, Oklahoma, a soft-spoken, mature student who showed us how to take adversity with good humor and how to be wise instead of smart alecks. Fraternity membership also taught me a lot about the power of group membership, the obligations, and the expectations from others that you would be loyal and could be counted on. It was an important growth experience that I would have missed had I stayed at home or lived in a dorm. The friendships I formed in DU lasted for decades, and the interpersonal education I gained is deeply embedded in me.

As far as figuring out what to do with my life, I floundered for two years, unable to decide what field to pursue. I felt I should try physics because Enrico Fermi gave incredibly interesting lectures in the one course that I took with him, but I was absolutely unable to do the problem sets and other homework that required a lot of math. This situation produced something of a crisis in that I was actually flunking physics. I did not want to create a family scandal by having an F on my record in my father's field. It was late in the semester, but I was able to do some heavy negotiating and convince the instructor to let me drop the course.

Carl Rogers

Because I could not decide what field to pursue, I stayed an extra year at Chicago and took more general education and humanities courses. Our general course in biological sciences covered aspects of psychology. Carl Rogers was on the Chicago faculty and had just begun to articulate his rather radical view of psychotherapy—people feel helped if you empathetically reflect back to them what they have just said. This not only sounded absurd at the time, when Freudian theory led to a therapeutic model of giving deep interpretations to a patient, but also lent itself wonderfully to caricature. Several of my friends and I had a grand old time practicing saying back to each other what the other had just said and then laughing derisively about this supposedly powerful therapeutic intervention.

The irony, of course, is that almost all my later work on process consultation and helping is entirely consistent with Rogerian principles, though this only became clear to me much later. I had to discover for myself that influencing others is very much a function of helping them to understand their own world and that this enables them in most cases to find their own solutions. Reflecting back to people what they said was merely a behavioral technique behind which stood a very important set of assumptions about human nature and how personal development takes place. During my time in Chicago and for decades thereafter, I never heard Rogers lecture, never met him, and never took his model seriously. Only in working on these memoirs have I realized how radical his thinking was in the 1940s.

Learning about psychology fed into the discovery that I wanted to do something very different from my father, so psychology seemed like the way to go. How I came to this decision is a bit of a mystery to me, and I have few recollections about the decision process and what my conversations with my parents about career choices and next schools might have been like. It was, however, taken for granted that I would continue my education and get a higher degree. In this respect, I followed in my father's footsteps.

Chicago did not have a strong psychology major. The work on the imprinting of young chicks was just beginning but did not really intrigue me, so I decided to pursue psychology elsewhere, and I found Stanford to be the best and most innovative in this field. The Hutchins program at Chicago issued bachelor's degrees after two years of study. My three years there earned me two of the Chicago-style degrees: a PhB (bachelor of philosophy) and a BA. The theory was that these should get you directly into a master's program, but this clearly was neither possible nor desirable since I had no solid major field. Learning psychology at Stanford and getting out of Chicago were obvious attractions, and the logical next steps, so I applied to Stanford, was admitted, and planned to go there as a senior in the fall of 1947.

Wisconsin Summers and Car Games (1942–47)

My life in the fraternity house was enhanced considerably by the fact that I acquired a car in 1945. One of my father's close friends, Sam Allison, was a professor of chemistry who had a big cottage in Wisconsin, to which he invited us for a week or two each summer. These were idyllic times of canoeing, rowing, fishing, mushroom picking, and generally enjoying this amazing region of interconnected lakes. However, I remember being surprised, shocked, and dismayed to see signs on restaurants that read, "No Jews allowed," reminding me of what my father had consistently worried about in urging me to change my name.

The Allisons had several cars. When I got to the driving age in 1945, Mrs. Allison offered to teach me to drive by letting me practice on the rural roads of Wisconsin. We used their '37 Chevrolet, and by some turn of fate, the Allisons offered to sell me the car for one hundred dollars at the end of the summer. A car was most welcome, as I was leaving home and moving into the fraternity. They drove the car back to Chicago and turned it over to me to get a license. Ever cautious, I wanted to do a lot more practicing, but several of my fraternity brothers coaxed me into going for the license right away. I still remember driving white-knuckled through the city streets to a Bureau of Motor Vehicles office, where I would take both the written and road tests. I thought my road test was suspiciously lax, but I passed and suddenly found myself free and with wheels.

In the meantime, my parents began to show an interest in having a car of their own. Marcel's fortunes at the university were rising—he was a full professor, he had his own lab, he was doing some consulting for General Electric, and he could now afford a car. They decided to buy a secondhand Lincoln-Zephyr instead of a new car so that my father could show off his growing status.

I was "employed" to teach my *mother* how to drive because, for various reasons, my father did not want to learn. For years, I had practiced teaching my parents about various aspects of US culture, so they were used to taking advice from me. Fortunately, my mother had good coordination, which made teaching her to drive quite feasible. She took to it and enjoyed the freedom that having a car provided. They could now travel more easily around the United States, and it also made it possible for my father to be driven to campus, even though it was less than a mile from our apartment to his office and he was in very good shape physically. His need for visible status led him to want to be driven but also led to his absurd insistence that he sit in the backseat while my mother gamely chauffeured him around!

The Lincoln made it possible to plan a big trip to Mexico in the spring of 1947. We would drive through Arkansas and Texas to Monterrey and all the way to Mexico City, where there was a physics congress that my father wanted to attend. Things went smoothly until we got to Little Rock, Arkansas, where the car had trouble and we learned that it needed a major engine overhaul, which would take at least a week. In order to get to the meetings, my father continued the trip by plane while my mother and I found ourselves stranded in Little Rock until the car got repaired.

The most memorable part of that trip was learning about dialects. We went through the mountains of Arkansas and stopped at a gas station. I had read about all kinds of bears in Yellowstone, and I wondered about the forests of Arkansas. So I marched up to the proprietor, who was sitting in his rocking chair puffing on a pipe, and asked, "Are there any bears around here?"

He said, "Yep, sure, lots of bears."

Curious, I pressed on, asking, "What kind of bears are they?" to which he answered, "Well, mostly blackbears and strawbears."

The Big Trip in the Summer of 1947

Life in the fraternity had given me a sense of independence, and I had a car to boot. I wanted to do something independent, to break away, to test myself. Stanford would start later in the fall, but that summer was wide-open. So I decided to go west by myself. I set off in my '37 Chevrolet with no clear destination or timetable in mind. In retrospect, this was quite unlike me. I had the courage or the foolhardiness of a nineteen-year-old. I don't know what my parents thought about this, but I did not care much because I had to honor my need to get out on my own.

I set off toward Rapid City, South Dakota. Soon after I left Chicago, I saw two young men hitchhiking, which was considered safe and acceptable in those days, with similar goals of taking a summer off to have adventures. They were brothers from a small town in Wisconsin who had some but not a lot of money for the trip and, like me, wanted to see more of the West. Joining up with them provided driving relief and welcome company.

As we cruised through the Midwest, we were deeply impressed by the flat plains of Iowa; by Mitchell, South Dakota, with its Corn Palace; by the Badlands of South Dakota; and by the grandeur of Mount Rushmore. But as we pushed on into Montana, we ran out of money, so it was time to find some work. This was bean-growing country, and farmhands were in high demand, so we were taken on for a week of hoeing beans.

Life on the farm was a new experience, quite different from the bucolic days of my youth in the mountains and in Wisconsin—early rising; an enormous breakfast; hours of nasty hoeing, which was upright work at least; fat sandwiches snarfed down for lunch; more hoeing; and then a huge dinner and collapsing into bed. The farm family was very amiable and supportive, which was a comfort, as I'm sure we weren't the most efficient workers they'd ever had.

Saturday nights involved a country ritual that was unlike anything I had ever experienced. There was a big hall in the nearest town, and all the young people came to it in their pickups and cars. All the boys lined up on one side, drinking Coke or beer that they had brought along, and the girls went to the other side, giggling and looking nervous. When the local country band struck up, the boys rushed over en masse to pick out the girl they had their eye on or, if she was not available, a second choice, or if they found no one who attracted them, they just kept on looking. Suddenly, the dance floor filled up with couples. When the music stopped, some boys and girls parted and went back to their respective sides while some pairs went outside to their cars for "necking." This ebb and flow went on for several hours. The music stopped near midnight, when everyone suddenly disappeared into their cars and trucks! The hall was completely empty within fifteen minutes.

After two weeks of hoeing, my two buddies from Wisconsin had earned enough for bus fare home, but I wanted to push on to Yellowstone Park. We parted with much self-congratulation for our achievements. It was good to know that a city slicker like me could hold his own in the fields. I entered Yellowstone at its north end at Mammoth Hot Springs, where there was a community consisting of a big hotel, a gas station, stores, and dormitories for all the employees of the hotel. I found the administrators there and asked about a job. It turned out that they needed someone at the gas station to pump gas, which was the perfect job for me—it was outdoors, I would meet lots of people, and best of all, I got to wear the green-and-white-striped Conoco uniform!

This was not my first experience of employment by a corporation. During my late high school years, I had worked at Carson Pirie Scott and Company, a large department store in downtown Chicago, selling men's shirts for a summer. That summer, I learned many things about sales organizations, about how to treat customers, and about competition among salespeople, which led to agreed-upon practices on the order in which we got to approach customers. Brief as these employment experiences were, they helped me to understand how selling shirts, hoeing beans, and pumping gas are fundamentally quite different processes.

Mammoth Hot Springs was a natural wonder. Everyone talks about Old Faithful and the geysers, but the multiple terraces of Mammoth, with their bubbling multicolored pools of boiling water, were every bit as amazing. Since I had the car, I could also visit the falls and other sites and make some extra money by offering to take park visitors on tours. It was on such trips with young families that I observed how utterly senseless human behavior could be. In spite of all the warnings, I consistently saw parents encourage their toddlers to get close to baby bears, even in the vicinity of the mother bears. Fortunately, nothing happened.

The many college students who served the hotel and resort area had rich social lives of their own, which not only made the whole experience pleasant but also introduced me to my first love: Carol Peterson. She was a senior at the University of Minnesota taking the summer off to work as a maid in the big hotel.

Carol was a few years older than I was, but we really hit it off and were quite in love. I had fallen in love twice before in Chicago in the sense that I found girls who were incredibly beautiful—one was unattainable because she was going steady with a friend; I dated the other one for a while, but the relationship did not deepen. With Carol, things were different. She not only attracted me physically, but we got along beautifully. We did not sleep together, however, because the 1947 norms about no intercourse until marriage were still pretty strong. Fraternity brothers bragged about making out, but this often turned out to be nothing more than heavy petting. We all lived with many fears and stereotypes about sex, masturbation, homosexuality, and venereal disease, fears that are largely gone as far as I can tell in observing my growing grandchildren. They know more, are less anxious about sex, and consequently are much more responsible in their handling of sex.

At the end of the summer, Carol and I made a plan that she would go back to finish college and I would go on to Stanford, but we promised to stay in touch. As I drove back to Chicago, I felt totally fulfilled by my western adventure. Looking back, I can hardly believe the things I did that summer given the tight rein that I had kept on myself in the previous years of acculturation. Having a car certainly helped me gain a sense of freedom and become that much more "American."

The important outcome of this summer was my confidence in striking out on my own. I felt thoroughly Americanized, I had been admitted to Stanford to study psychology, and I had a car and a girlfriend. I was also only nineteen and, in retrospect, quite immature. But I was in the right place at the right time and able to be creatively opportunistic in this next period of my life. I finally knew what I wanted to do—enter a field completely different from my father's. Psychology fit that bill nicely, and Stanford's quarter system provided a golden opportunity to fulfill the requirements for a bachelor's degree in one calendar year.

Chapter 4
Stanford (1947–49)

At the end of the summer of 1947, I packed up my Chevrolet and drove across the southern United States, sleeping in my car and occasionally stopping at motels along the way. Driving through the Southwest, I experienced those famed qualities of its "big sky" and "open road," which gave me a wonderful sense of adventure. Upon arrival at Stanford, I was immediately taken by the campus with its yellow sandstone architecture and palm trees. The university was still known as the "farm" then and was ensconced in lush groves of apricot and plum trees. Especially striking to me was the contrast between the total Midwestern flatness of Chicago and the foothills one saw both to the east and to the west of the Stanford campus. The peninsula, now Silicon Valley, with San Francisco at one end and San Jose at the other end, was uniquely beautiful.

I lived in some temporary dorms in Menlo Park for a while and then in a regular two-person room on campus, where I met Hamad al-Khalifa, one of the princes of the Bahrain royal family. We became good friends, but unfortunately, I lost touch with Hamad after graduate school. I never learned about his progress in the royal succession, but it impressed me that, in the 1940s, the Arab sheikhdoms were making a serious effort to educate their future rulers in Western schools. I also learned another intercultural lesson when, one afternoon, Hamad asked me to wake him from a nap. I gently touched him on his side only to have him practically take my arm off as he jumped, rotated, and chopped down hard on the "threatening object that was touching him." He warned me never to touch him because he would instinctively and automatically take it as a threat.

At Chicago, I had enjoyed the fraternity life and done well enough in my classes, but clearly I had drifted. At Stanford, I found myself totally focused, devouring my courses and enjoying complete absorption in the subject and all its variations. Carol and I continued our relationship by correspondence while she finished her senior year at Minnesota. This arrangement made it easy for me to commit totally to classes and my studies. I don't recall what I did for lunches, but for most dinners, I went to the Peninsula Creamery in Palo Alto for a cheeseburger with fries and a chocolate malt. Fresh apricots and plums for dessert were plentiful.

I did not have much time for tennis and did not really like the hard courts after learning on clay, but in the winter months, I discovered the incredibly good skiing that could be had even into the spring months in the Sierras. There is nothing so uplifting and dramatic as to be in the upper reaches of Yosemite contemplating your downhill run in your shirtsleeves in the bright sunshine of mid-April. Life in California was good.

Psychology had clearly been the right choice, and social psychology turned out to be a good focus for me within the discipline. Although I was not really conscious of this focus at the time, in retrospect, it seems that I needed to learn more about myself in relation to others and to understand interpersonal influence better. So much of life is interpersonal yet mysterious. I was ready to find out what I could learn and how it could be demystified.

I was able to take enough courses in four quarters to fulfill the major requirements, which, along with my three years at Chicago, qualified me for a legitimate BA. All that I was learning excited me so much that I decided to continue attending Stanford for a master's degree. This decision was reinforced largely by the arrival of Visiting Professor Harry Helson, who needed an assistant for his social influence experiments with perceptions of weight. I also became a teaching assistant in statistics for Quinn McNemar, which I proudly emphasize on my resume to prove to myself and the world that failure in physics does not mean utter incompetence in math.

Learning theory was coming into its own under Ernest Hilgard, a phenomenal lecturer, and because of visits from another giant in the field, Edward Tolman, who was doing his classic rat maze experiments at Berkeley. Experimental psychology using rats was very much alive. For example, important studies were discovering how rats developed cognitive maps of their mazes and made systematic errors. When I am heading for a particular well-known street and turn prematurely down the one preceding the correct one, I am reminded that this phenomenon was well demonstrated in the anticipatory response that rats consistently made in their efforts to find the correct turn for food in the maze.

The abnormal psychology course under Calvin Stone allowed my friends and me to self-diagnose ourselves with every kind of psychological affliction described in the books. I learned later that seeing pathology in oneself is a typical student reaction, and in a way, we reveled in it. I learned about social psychology from another excellent teacher, Paul Farnsworth, and used the social psychology text by Krech and Crutchfield, which became a classic in the field and still occupies an important place on my bookshelves.

Child development also interested me, and therein lies another story. Carol had finished her BA at the University of Minnesota and decided to get a job in Palo Alto so that she could join me again. We were in love, but in the 1940s, it would not have been appropriate to live together. While I continued in my own room, she rented a room in the house of Professor Al Baez, a friend of my father. He had a big house and two daughters whom I met—eight-year-old Joan and three-year-old Mimi.

As part of my child development class, we had to find a young child to interview to determine what his or her sense of causality was. For example, we would ask him or her why the clouds in the sky move. Mimi Baez was the perfect subject, and I spent hours chatting with her for my report. Many years later, I learned that her older sister, whom I had also gotten to know, became the acclaimed singer Joan Baez. I also learned that Mimi had died after a very successful singing career of her own.

One of my good friends at Stanford was Allen Newell, a physics major who later became well known in the field of artificial intelligence as a professor at Carnegie Mellon University. Some of his friends and I spent many hours on parapsychology, which was in vogue because of experiments at Duke University that claimed to prove the existence of not only extrasensory perception (ESP) but psychokinesis—the ability to move things with psychological forces—as well.

As a physics major, Allen was able to construct a perfectly flat glass table. For many hours, several of us would sit around this table and concentrate with all our might to make a highly polished ball bearing move off its position at the center of the table. The friction was minimal, our mental efforts were prodigious, but alas, the marble never moved. The enormous energy that Newell and his friends spent on this project did not surprise me because I had known from my earlier days among University of Chicago physicists, especially the theoretical ones like Fermi, that parapsychology fascinated them and that, in a way, they wanted to believe in it. Too bad the marble didn't move.

My First Experiment in Social Psychology

Muzafer Sherif and Solomon Asch's social influence experiments were not only fascinating; they also fed into my early interest in interpersonal dynamics. What people saw was influenced by the reports of others even when the others were, by the experimenter's instructions, giving incorrect responses. How and why does such social influence occur? Little did I know at the time that I would encounter the real thing a few years later in my involvement with the repatriation of ex-POWs from Chinese and North Korean POW camps.

What Harry Helson wanted to do, using me as a research assistant, fell squarely in this area. He had developed a mathematical theory of adaptation level, showing experimentally that if we are first exposed to a range of light stimuli, we evolve a neutral point above which we feel that a given light is bright and below which we feel it is dim. Helson would expose subjects to different levels of light and then ask them to rate the lights as being bright or dim. He would then show that the neutral point above which people said "bright" or below which they said "dim" could be influenced by first showing a reference light. If the reference light was very bright, subjects would later report much brighter levels as being dim, whereas if the reference light shown first was quite dim, those same other levels would later be reported as being bright. The reference light anchored the scale and created a new subjective scale and a new adaptation level.

This phenomenon is well understood and used in all sorts of practical ways. For example, a manager who wants to cut expenses by 5 percent and knows that he or she will encounter all kinds of arguments about what can be cut announces that cost cutting in the 10 to 15 percent range will probably be coming, thereby providing a high anchor. Invariably, the 5 percent cut is achieved with much less objection. Stores use this principle when they announce drastic sales, such as 75 percent off the original price, but make the original price so high that the customer will still pay a lot and yet believe he or she is getting a bargain. Our judgments are usually based on the points of reference, the anchoring stimulus, and not some absolute standard.

Helson had shown the same phenomenon with weight judgments of "heavy" and "light" and now wondered if the judgment would also be influenced by a reference weight or anchor that was *social* in nature. In his classic experiments, Asch had shown that some subjects could be influenced to report two lines that were *obviously* unequal in length to be equal if previous subjects who were confederates of the experimenter had deliberately chosen the obviously wrong line as the correct match. It appeared that under social pressure, many subjects would rather falsify what they saw than challenge their peers' perceptions. We wanted to explore to what degree judgments of heaviness could be influenced by hearing the judgments of others before one made one's own. Helson wanted to show that the reference anchors could be social as well as physical.

We constructed a box into which one reached so that one could not see the actual weights. Subjects were then asked to pick up a weight and declare whether it felt heavy or light. Each subject judged a whole series of weights alone so that we could determine at what weight level he or she switched a judgment from heavy to light. Then, instead of providing new reference weights to shift the scale, we started to test subjects in pairs. One member of each pair was always a confederate of the experimenter with specific instructions on when to shift. He or she always responded first. Not surprisingly, we found that hearing another person's prior judgments strongly influenced the experimental subjects' judgments. I wrote up this experiment for my master's thesis and thereby officially launched my career as an experimental social psychologist with a specific interest in the mechanisms of social influence.

This field rapidly grew as psychologists were trying to understand what had happened in Nazi Germany and in American race relations. How could one explain the horrific programs of genocide in Nazi Germany and the continued segregation, lynchings, and general levels of race prejudice in the United States? In each case, a central question was how seemingly ordinary people could be made to do such obviously evil things. Political, social, and interpersonal influence each had to be understood, fueling many research programs that, in a sense, created the field of social psychology and group dynamics.

Experimental studies of group dynamics, social influence, responses to authority, leadership styles, and related phenomena were funded both by foundations and by the US government through the research arms of the army, navy, and air force. A number of European social psychologists had emigrated and were founding research programs in the United States, notably Kurt Lewin, whose work on social change had been influential during the war.

Planning the Future

I decided that experimental social psychology was the field for me because I could now see how one could actually do laboratory experiments to explore the mysterious process of how social influence occurs. What remained was to get a PhD and join academia. Though Stanford's department was strong, I had already taken almost all the courses available. It was time to look elsewhere. The University of Michigan had a very strong department in group dynamics and social psychology, and Harvard had just created the Department of Social Relations, which included anthropology, sociology, clinical psychology, and social psychology. The senior professors in each of these fields had decided that it would be important to work together and to separate themselves collectively from Harvard's more traditional psychology department, which was oriented toward the study of sensation and perception.

I applied to both departments and got accepted by both. Michigan recruited me more actively, with ethically questionable, premature offers of financial aid, but Harvard's broader program and its name convinced me to go there in the fall of 1949. I drove my '37 Chevrolet back to Chicago to prepare for the big move east. This time, I was leaving Chicago and my parents for good.

Doing It My Own Way: Who Are We Really?

The decision to go to Harvard was easy, but the decision about my relationship with Carol was more difficult. As I finished my time at Stanford, we decided to get married at the end of the summer and go on to Cambridge together. Carol would go back to Minnesota to get ready, though no formal date had been set. I drove back to Chicago full of excitement about my future PhD study. Even during the drive home, I noticed that I was much more thrilled about Harvard than about getting married.

I had not informed my parents about my marital intentions. When I broke the news to them, they were shocked and somewhat skeptical about the wisdom of the decision to get married at this time. They reminded me that I was only twenty-one and in the middle of my education. They had not met Carol, and they were offended that they had not been involved in the decision. All these questions woke me up. What was I thinking? I had been passively going with the flow in my personal life, enjoying the comfort of having a girlfriend and a plan for the future, but the decision to get a PhD had made me realize that I had to reevaluate my priorities. What in the world was I doing, getting married as I entered an exciting PhD program?

Not surprisingly, the plan to get married unraveled during the summer. I wrote Carol a long but resolute letter terminating the relationship. I felt ashamed and guilty. Carol did not take it well, but I felt more and more confident about the decision. I had loved her company and appreciated her friendship, but we did not have enough deep love or common ground to sustain a marriage at that point. So I packed up for Cambridge and a new life.

A question I now ask myself is whether I took advantage of Carol. Did part of me know all along that I would not get married at this stage? Why did Carol and I agree to get married but not set a date? Why had I not met her parents, nor she mine? In retrospect, our plan was pretty flimsy. Regardless of how young and immature we were, I must have sent some signals along the way that I was more interested in my own career than in settling down.

Writing her a letter from Chicago now strikes me as blatantly avoiding a likely painful face-to-face confrontation. It also strikes me as caring far more for my own comfort than for Carol's feelings. I felt guilty, but not guilty enough to go see her and convey my feelings. I wanted at that point just to escape from the relationship and get on with my academic studies. Some twenty-five years later, I received a letter from Carol revealing that she was married, had several children, and was not harboring a grudge. I admit this letter was welcome in that it reduced my guilt somewhat. But what was the basis of this guilt?

I had been afraid that I would hurt her, and I now realized that this was based on the automatic assumption that I have the power to hurt. Attributing power to oneself is really quite arrogant when one thinks about it. It made me aware that, along with the cautious, lonely only child, there coexists in me another only child who feels privileged, omnipotent, and deserving. Even as I timidly make my way into new and strange situations, I applaud myself for how well I am doing it.

What strikes me is the easy coexistence of caution, shame, and guilt with arrogance and self-congratulation. I always feel in danger that I am doing something wrong, that I will be shamed, and that I have unacceptable feelings and impulses, yet at the same time, I can feel confident and very proud of how well I am doing, how clever I am, and how creative my productions are. I can at once feel guilty for how insensitive I was to Carol and feel entitled to do what's best for me.

Is this the outcome of mothering that provides constant praise for every little accomplishment, coupled with occasional unexpected slaps to the back of the head and very punishing words? It was an important discovery for me that quite contradictory feelings can so comfortably coexist—that I have multiple selves that are always active and can be drawn upon in different situations. I am much more attracted to sociological theories of the self, which emphasize that as we grow up, we develop layers and layers of selves, all of which make up who we are. Personality theories that type us as one thing or another are all well and good, but they tend to oversimplify. Even as I write these memoirs, I see new facets of myself that derive from different life experiences.

Seeing these multiple selves within me also makes me quite impatient with personality theories and developmental theories that characterize us as having achieved different levels of maturity. I can see different personalities and levels of maturity in how I operate in different situations and resist efforts to hang a single label on myself.

Chapter 5
Harvard and the Army
(1949–52)

At the end of the summer of 1949, I once again set off in my '37 Chevrolet for Cambridge and Harvard. I found a room on Ellery Street a few blocks from Emerson Hall, which was to be my academic home for three years. I liked Cambridge immediately, especially the urban excitement of Harvard Square with its "cafeterias" Albiani's and Hayes-Bickford's, the Wursthaus, and the Harvard Coop, with its multifaceted bookstore. For the first time, I found myself in a truly urban scene and in a more academic environment.

Both Chicago and Stanford had been self-contained campuses from which one could go downtown or into San Francisco, so I was well acquainted with urban life, but Harvard sprawled into the surrounding community, which resulted in more bookshops, cafés, and movie theaters being right there within a few square blocks. Harvard had adopted an architectural policy of building in the contemporary style, so one saw in Harvard Yard a hodgepodge of everything from seventeenth-century wooden buildings to a super modern Le Corbusier arts center.

Cambridge itself was an industrial city of 250,000 that just happened to have within its boundaries two great universities, a bunch of smaller colleges, and a growing research establishment. The contrast between Harvard and the Gothic splendor of Chicago and the beautiful yellow stone "farm" of Stanford was profound. And the contrasts within the Harvard area itself were equally profound in that one could find complete tranquility inside of Harvard Yard or along the Charles River or, alternatively, mingle with hundreds of high schoolers who found Harvard Square, at that time the end of the subway line, to be full of excitement.

For me, there was even a little bit of Europe in that the Wursthaus had respectable German food and beer, while a block away, there was the Window Shop, a world-class bakery and coffeehouse run by a group of Viennese ladies who gave the proceeds of the shop to Jewish refugees of the Holocaust. The Cambridge scene was new and different and exciting.

Coming east was a new cultural adjustment on several levels, most evident to me in the semantics of food. A cafeteria, I learned, was actually a high counter behind which stood two or three men in front of a kitchen. The food options were posted on the wall above them, you ordered, they shouted the order to the kitchen, and in due course, they gave you the platter you had ordered. I had a hard time choosing something that I could not see, violating the very essence of what a cafeteria was supposed to make possible, but I soon got the hang of it from looking at the other plates that appeared on the counter. You then took your plate to a booth or table and sometimes found colleagues eating there as well. Albiani's was famous for the fact that Paul Samuelson apparently wrote the first edition of his famed economics text over breakfasts there. I also learned that when I ordered my standard dinner of a cheeseburger with fries and a malted milkshake, I would get no ice cream in the drink unless I asked for a frappe.

I was once again independent and doing something new, a feeling that I loved, but I was also acutely aware that I was making a major commitment for the next six to eight years. In late 1949, the draft was still operating, and I realized that if I got drafted, I would lose all my educational momentum. I learned that the US Army was offering a clinical psychology training program that would enlist you as a second lieutenant and pay for the rest of your PhD program in exchange for three years of service in the regular army following completion of the PhD. The main attraction of this program, besides the financial benefit, was I would spend my time in the regular army as a psychologist. If I got drafted, there was no telling what I would end up doing. So I applied for this program, got accepted, and thereby, without realizing it at the time, changed the course of my career and life. I had no way of knowing how my involvement with the army would lead to my work with Korean POW repatriates and how this would start weaning me away from pure experimental social psychology, which, at this point, was my total passion.

My entering the army enormously pleased my father because he felt that the United States had been very good to him and my military service was, in a sense, paying the country back. This was, of course, ironic, as his own parents had sent him to study physics to avoid military service in World War I. It was very enlightened of the US Army to have created programs that supported education, which thereby guaranteed bringing professions into the army for at least a period of time.

Entering the army as a graduate student was bizarre. When my letter of acceptance arrived, it instructed me to go to the US Army Headquarters in downtown Boston to be sworn in and to receive further instructions. A friendly but stern sergeant told me to buy *The Officers Guide*, to order uniforms by mail, and to stand in front of a mirror to learn to salute. I would not have to wear a uniform while in graduate school, but I had to be ready for future assignments. I would require no special training, but I was admonished to study the training manual carefully. I was sworn in and given my gold second lieutenant's bars and my Medical Service Corps pins to put on my uniform when it arrived. Last, but certainly not least, I signed for my monthly salary, which was more than most graduate student stipends.

The Unique Nature of the Social Relations Department

I had arrived at Harvard at a unique time in its history. The leaders of several major social science departments—clinical psychology under Henry Murray, social psychology under Gordon Allport, sociology under Talcott Parsons and Sam Stouffer, and anthropology under Clyde Kluckhohn—had decided to form one Department of Social Relations (SocRel), formally split off from the regular Psychology Department. Along with this senior group came a number of others who were already or would later become eminent faculty members—Fried Bales, Roger Brown, Jerome Bruner, George Homans, Florence Kluckhohn, David McClelland, Richard Solomon, and Robert White, to name a few. Each graduate student could concentrate in one of the major fields but would have to take courses in each of the other fields as well.

The impact of this curricular shift was enormous. With departmental offices and seminar rooms consolidated in Emerson Hall, faculty and graduate students from different fields were thrust together. The third floor had a large oval table where we met every day for lunch, making new friends across disciplines as we took advantage of the free make-your-own-sandwich spread. We were thrilled to eavesdrop as faculty members from the different departments engaged in lively discussion and debate during these lunches, and later, several of them cotaught courses. The most important discovery of this academic diversification was the interest our faculty mentors displayed in trying to broaden their and our thinking. Interdisciplinary thinking was clearly touted as the way of the future in social sciences. I found this very satisfying and am nowadays disturbed that I increasingly see a pull in the opposite direction, each field becoming more quantitative and separate, evolving its own jargon and favorite research methods.

By the end of the first semester, I knew two other students well enough to move into a three-bedroom apartment on Concord Avenue with them—Geoff Caston, who was actually in political science but taking many of the SocRel courses, and Joe Kahl, who was a second-year sociology student studying the US social-class structure. This mixture of intellectual interests forced us to truly appreciate the contribution of each field to a given phenomenon, and it made for more than a handful of late-night debates. The course work was interesting, my graduate student friends were stimulating, and I was getting excellent mentoring from Gordon Allport, learning especially about his passion for good writing. He stated flatly, "If you can't write it, you don't know it," a principle that I never forgot and that I passed on to my own students.

A Potpourri of SocRel Research

Some of the work going on in SocRel and in our neighboring Psychology Department during these years is worth noting for its zaniness. B. F. Skinner was evolving his operant conditioning theories by demonstrating how rewards shape behavior. Not only was this highly relevant to training dogs and other animals, but Skinner got a lot of publicity teaching pigeons to peck at a Ping-Pong ball so that two pigeons could peck it back and forth across the Ping-Pong table. I still remember his concluding announcement after months of pigeon training: "Yes, pigeons can learn to play Ping-Pong, but not very well." Skinner had also developed the

"Skinner box" for training infants, but this involved a degree of physical separation of infant from mother that became highly controversial. A lot of research evidence in psychology and anthropology showed that intimate physical contact was important at an early age. Even though the Skinner box would make the training of an infant more efficient, it was viewed as too damaging to emotional development.

Learning theory has always been one of the pillars of psychology, and we all realized how important Skinnerian behaviorism was to understanding human behavior. Instead of punishing unwanted behavior, as Pavlovian conditioning had advocated, *you should ignore it* and let it atrophy. Punishing bad behavior may not only harm the psyche but also teach the child how to get attention when he or she wants it. You could then explain neurotic compulsive behavior by the secondary gain that the patient gets from attention. This principle was very new at the time but has become the bedrock of animal training. It led to a refined way of thinking about discipline—only punish when immediate harm will come from the behavior.

Psychoanalytic theory was alive and well but under fire for lack of empirical evidence for key concepts such as ego, id, and superego. Richard Solomon was hard at work to test one aspect of the theory by examining the evolution of these structures. We pretty much knew that humans could differentiate shame from guilt and, therefore, had a superego. If you did something inappropriate in the presence of others and felt horrible about it, that was *shame*. If you did the same thing but there was no one else around to witness it and you still felt horrible about it, that was *guilt*, which reflected the superego or conscience.

I never found out why Dick Solomon wanted to test this in dogs, but that was indeed his project. Did dogs have a superego? To test this experimentally, dogs were put into a situation where they would have to defecate in a forbidden area. In condition 1, the dog had an audience and, as predicted, showed all kinds of shameful and fearful behavior—looking around anxiously and cowering. In condition two, the dog was alone but observed by a hidden camera. The results were decisive. When alone, the dog did *not* show any signs of distress after pooping. Only when people showed up did the fearful behavior occur. So dogs have shame but no guilt.

Many of us thought this might have been a bit off the charts as a use of expensive lab resources, but in this same lab, Solomon was doing a more significant project on aspects of Pavlovian conditioning and the development of addictive neurotic behavior. In this experiment, a divider, over which a dog could jump, separated two boxes. The floor was electrified in each box so that the experimenter could administer shocks. The idea was to teach the dog to jump into the other box in anticipation of being shocked when a bell rang. Once the dog learned this, it was then complicated by ringing the bell in the second box prior to administering a shock there. So, of course, the dog would jump back into the first box until a bell was rung there, causing back-and-forth jumping in response to the bell. The shocks could now be turned off in both boxes, and the dog would continue to jump back and forth every time the bell rang, even to the point of exhaustion, and never discover that no more shocks occurred. Whatever one thought of the import of these findings, or the abuse of animals, I learned how one could elegantly design and execute a straightforward psychological experiment from this.

From my experiences with Harry Helson at Stanford and Richard Solomon at Harvard, I learned how to be an experimental social psychologist and grew to admire this field hugely. I developed close mentoring relationships with Gordon Allport, who embodied carefully thought-out theory presented elegantly in writing, and with Solomon, who represented genius in the design and execution of experiments. Both eventually became my dissertation advisors.

In the meantime, there was much to absorb from the rest of the faculty. Henry Murray and David McClelland were in the midst of working out the use of the Thematic Apperception Test (TAT). Talcott Parsons was working out his grand theory of social action, which provided us with endless opportunities for caricature, as he would say things in the most abstract, pedantic way possible and frequently change his theory.

George Homans was writing his definitive theory of social exchange and group dynamics, while Fried Bales was studying the evolution of roles in group meetings by carefully observing experimentally created groups. He discovered that groups evolve both a *task* leader and a *socioemotional* leader, and they are usually different people. Sam Stouffer was analyzing the massive surveys of "The American Soldier" and showing us all the power of survey-based research.

Florence Kluckhohn and Fred Strodtbeck were developing the interviews and questionnaires that would be used later in their classic comparative study of the four cultures that coexisted at the Four Corners area of southeast

Utah. Clyde Kluckhohn and Evan Vogt were sending their graduate students to live with the Navajos, which would yield countless humorous accounts of the trials and tribulations of fieldwork in the US southwest. Kluckhohn also headed the Russian Research Center, which brought together a variety of faculty from SocRel and political science, notably Alex Inkeles and Ray Bauer, who became highly valued Russian experts during the Cold War. Gordon Allport and Leo Postman's study of rumor became a classic. All of us were preoccupied in one way or another with trying to explain Nazism and the psychosocial phenomena of war.

Of greatest interest to me was the work of Jerry Bruner on the influence of social class on perception. He showed kids from various socioeconomic strata brief exposures of coins and asked them to match what they saw to a disk whose size they could change. Poorer kids saw coins as larger than richer kids did! Although Sherif, Asch, and others showed that subjects would report incorrect perceptions because they buckled to social pressure, we never doubted that their eyes *saw* things correctly. The Bruner experiment suggested that motivational and emotional factors would actually influence what the eye perceived.

I learned later from experiments with hearing that the perceptual system is not a passive tabula rasa recording data but an active process of seeking out and paying attention to the things that concern us. Perception is a motivated process subject to all kinds of biases. That partly explains why artists must expend so much energy in learning to see what is actually out there before they can attempt to draw or paint it with any degree of accuracy.

In the meantime, my apartment mate, Joe Kahl, was

studying a related phenomenon. Harvard gave scholarships to high school students from lower-socioeconomic strata but had observed that many of them nevertheless decided not to come to Harvard. For his dissertation research, Kahl interviewed a sample of those who enrolled and compared them to a matched sample who were admitted but did not come in order to find out what led them to opt out. The results were quite clear. If the father said, in effect, "Congratulations, son, but why would you want to go to Harvard anyway? Isn't what I do good enough for you? You want to be better, eh?" the likelihood of the kid coming to Harvard was small. If the father said, "That's wonderful! You should try to get an education so that you can do better than I did," then his son was likely to attend. Simple but true, parental attitudes are a powerful influence on the course of a child's life.

Not everything going on in SocRel was benign. LSD had been discovered, and Timothy Leary was beginning to form a group of adventuresome graduate students who would take the drug in order to study its effects. As we now know, the problem was that the effects, however interesting, do not always wear off. Years later, I learned from fellow alumni of incidents where they had "tripped out" without warning and that they often felt that "they were never quite the same again." They did the research with plenty of supports in place during the initial trials, but even then, I remember finding out that some of my friends were sent home while still under the influence.

In the clinical area, the study of human motivation picked up steam. Nazism had spurred a great deal of research on the nature of authority, marked by the landmark publication of *The Authoritarian Personality*. With the help of the TAT, Murray and McClelland were formulating a basic typology of motives that would explain the phenomena of leadership, management, and entrepreneurship. The needs for power, achievement, and affiliation or social connection were considered the primary motives of all humans, and an analysis of the stories that a person told based on the ambiguous TAT cards could measure their relative strength.

The authoritarian personality was defined by a rigid concern for power down and up. This kind of person had a very low tolerance for ambiguity, was both respectful and subservient to superiors, and was very arbitrary in asserting authority over subordinates. The measurement of tolerance for ambiguity illustrated the admirable cleverness of the experimenters. A series of drawings would be shown to the subject in very short exposures so that they were never completely clear. The drawings started as clear silhouettes of a cat, went through several stages of nebulous transition, and ended up looking exactly like a dog. For each brief exposure, the subject was asked what he or she saw.

A person highly tolerant of ambiguity would report a sequence like the following: "Cat, cat, getting blurry, not sure, starting to look like something else, still blurry, looks like a dog, dog, dog." A person low in tolerance would say, "Cat, cat, cat, *cat*, *cat*, my God, it's a dog, dog, dog," and would exhibit real signs of stress while looking at the ambiguous drawings. The grand hypothesis was that the German character was a prototype of the authoritarian personality, which would explain why so many people accepted orders to do unthinkably cruel and inhumane things.

However, the startling and now iconic series of experiments later executed by Stanley Milgram at Yale showed that in a random selection of adults, approximately one-third would take orders from the experimenter to give what they believed to be dangerously high electric shocks to a fellow subject in the experiment if he or she made mistakes in a simulated learning task. However much one believed in "national character," Milgram showed that even in the United States, the social pressure caused by someone in authority commanding us to do something that might harm another is much more powerful than we know.

The ultimate explanation of the Nazi horror would rest ultimately in a combination of economics, history, sociology, and psychology, but an unanticipated consequence of the Milgram experiments was that they changed experimental psychology forever. The psychological effects on the experimental subjects—the discovery that they were capable of truly hurting another when ordered to—were considered damaging to these subjects. This prompted the introduction of informed-consent rules: you could not dupe subjects if possible harm was involved, you had to get their consent and explain the experiment, and if research funding was involved, the design had to be approved by a committee that examined the ethical implications of the experiment. Even what I had done at Stanford would have been challenged because we were subjecting students to social influence without their consent or knowledge, and the discovery that they had given in to such influence could potentially harm their self-image.

The McClelland–Murray theory that all of us are combinations of the need for power, the need for affiliation, and the need for achievement was widely accepted, and various patterns could then be correlated with leadership and entrepreneurship. One of the interesting findings that emerged was that leaders and managers were more motivated by power, while entrepreneurs were more motivated by a need for achievement. Economists had shown that economic development was correlated with local entrepreneurship, leading McClelland to propose that if one stimulated the need for achievement, this would stimulate entrepreneurship and, consequently, future economic development. He tested this notion in underdeveloped countries by teaching need for achievement to encourage local entrepreneurship. As far as I can recall, development organizations expended considerable effort but reaped minimal results. Though this extrapolation was not highly successful, the basic tripartite motivation model became a cornerstone of motivation theory, and the TAT took its place alongside the Rorschach as a basic projective test of personality.

Studies that covered several fields were also being undertaken. One of the most significant examined child-rearing methods in different cultures and the impact of parental behavior on personality outcomes in children. Beatrice and John Whiting created a large cross-cultural study of child-rearing methods, which then led to a study of parental behavior conducted by Robert Sears and Eleanor Maccoby.

The lunches at Emerson Hall were, for me, a great magnet. It excited me to meet faculty frequently and informally, and the discussions that arose were engaging and fruitful. Clyde Kluckhohn had a similar lunch option at his Russian Research Center, and the clinical psychologists often congregated at a house where Murray, White, McClelland, and others had their offices and seminars. Years later, Kluckhohn was asked what it took to run a center like his, and he answered, without hesitation, "It takes a building and a free lunch."

Internship at Walter Reed Hospital

The SocRel PhD program required some kind of fieldwork or internship. Since I was in the Army Clinical Psychology Program, I had a fairly easy time arranging an internship in the psychiatric ward at the Walter Reed Army Medical Center in Washington, DC. This, however, required being on a military post as a second lieutenant, and that, in turn, meant donning the uniform and learning at least the basics of military rules. I had purchased *The Officers Guide* and glanced at it from time to time, but now it suddenly required serious study, as I did not want to embarrass myself on the grounds of Walter Reed.

I can recall the absurdity of having to train myself for an organization that was so formal and rule-bound. The gold bars for my collar and the Medical Service Corps insignia had to be attached just so; the shirt, tie, trousers, and jacket had to be properly coordinated; and most important of all, I had to learn how to salute properly because I would encounter officers and enlisted men on the Walter Reed grounds. Learning to salute without coaching took careful reading of the manual and then standing in front of a mirror to practice over and over. I did not want to show up at Walter Reed looking like the amateur that I was.

Somehow, I got myself to Walter Reed, reported for

duty, and got assigned to the ward as a psychologist, ready to give tests to patients as requested by the psychiatrists. I did not have special training in test analysis but learned fairly quickly from experience that some of the important diagnostics were derived from the Rorschach inkblots, the TAT stories, and the Wechsler Bellevue Intelligence Test. I had a good teacher, Jim Lawrence, a civilian clinical psychologist employed by Walter Reed, who taught me the basics of forming a relationship with a patient, administering the tests required by the psychiatrist in charge of the case, diagnosing the results, and writing them up in a suitable form for the patient's records. I must admit I felt pretty important doing a real job in a real-life situation. I found hearing what people actually saw on a Rorschach blot extremely interesting, and being able to handle the testing situation gave me confidence that I could be a psychologist.

Data Gathering for My Dissertation

The internship period at Walter Reed also provided an opportunity to gather data for my dissertation. My continuing interests in social influence led me to conduct an experimental study of imitation for my doctorate. If people learned to imitate someone performing one task, would they continue to imitate on a different task? To test this, I needed groups of subjects who would, one person at a time and in turn, give their estimate of how many dots they saw on a slide that was exposed for a short period of time.

I worked with groups of five so that I could consistently choose one person's answer as the correct one. The goal was to establish the second subject in the response order as correct most of the time in order to see whether the third, fourth, and fifth subjects would learn to imitate him. After enough trials indicated that subject number two was being imitated, I switched to three new tasks that were also ambiguous but less and less similar to the original one. For example, in the third task, I showed them sets of five photographs and asked them to judge which was the prettiest.

Getting enough college students to do this was going to be problematic, but close to Walter Reed was an army induction center that processed draftees for military service. I found a room in the center and arranged for two groups of five men in the morning and two groups of five men in the afternoon to report to me as part of their induction process. From their point of view, it was just one of many tests that inductees were subjected to. My testing was harmless, so it did not require special debriefing. After a couple of months, I had tested 240 subjects and collected all my dissertation data. I returned to Cambridge ready for the task of writing my thesis.

The data clearly revealed that people would learn to imitate someone who was shown to be correct on many trials of an ambiguous task and would continue to imitate on a similar task, but not on a different task. I was very proud to have conducted an experiment that demonstrated clear results and, at the same time, felt very fortunate to have been able to gather my data in such an expeditious manner. The ease of getting experimental subjects in this way stood in sharp contrast to the difficulty of getting college sophomores to volunteer. Using army inductees also assured a somewhat more random sample of subjects. This bit of creative opportunism probably saved me an entire year in my PhD program.

In the Meantime: Doug McGregor, Kurt Lewin, and the MIT Research Center for Group Dynamics

I was not aware during my first two years at Harvard that a momentous program had been operating down the river at MIT. Doug McGregor, who got his PhD in psychology from Harvard in 1937, had become a professor in the MIT Department of Economics and Social Studies, which had developed a management track that included psychology and an industrial relations section that Doug headed until 1948. Doug's own field was research on leadership, so when, in 1948, he was recruited to be president of Antioch College, he accepted, he said, in order to test out some of his own theories. Before his departure, he had been instrumental in building up the psychology side in the management track and in helping to bring Kurt Lewin to MIT.

Lewin, the famous German émigré social psychologist, had been doing seminal research at Iowa and had expressed some interest in coming to Harvard, but for inexplicable reasons, Harvard could not accommodate him. Gordon Allport asked Doug McGregor whether there might be a position for Lewin at MIT, and they managed to bring him to Cambridge in 1945. Lewin immediately attracted a set of graduate students and created a Research Center for Group Dynamics that spawned most of the major figures in that field. One of these was Alex Bavelas, who had taken a job as an assistant professor at the MIT School of Industrial Management. Until 1952, MIT had only granted undergraduate degrees in management. With a large grant from the Sloan Foundation, MIT created a graduate program offering a master's degree in management.

Bavelas was offering a graduate course in group dynamics, which I was able to attend in 1950, since Harvard and MIT had cross-registration opportunities. His ability to stimulate excitement and his creativity in the design of experiments were unbelievable, as was best illustrated by what became the classic one-way, two-way communication experiment. One person is put in front of a group of any size and told to verbally instruct the group to reproduce a diagram that the group could not see. Using different but comparable groups and diagrams, this was to be done under three different conditions: (1) one-way, in which only the presenter could speak; (2) partial two-way, in which the group members could signal whether they understood or not with a yes or no; and (3) full two-way, in which the group could ask questions and get as much clarification as needed.

Bavelas measured how long it would take to finish the task and how accurate the group products were. The more the group was allowed to talk, the longer it took. But the accuracy results were surprising—condition one was clearly the worst. No matter how carefully the instructions were given, many mistakes occurred in almost every reproduction. In condition two, accuracy was much better. Condition three was better yet, but it took so much longer that one had to consider whether the extra accuracy was worth it. Condition two, the limited feedback option, was clearly the best choice for what was needed.

I learned later that this experiment was fueled by the practical Cold War need to design communication systems for bomb shelters in case of nuclear attacks. The one-way system would be inexpensive in that one could install a loudspeaker and just send instructions, but clearly the risk that the instructions would not be understood was serious. The full two-way would not only be expensive because it would require a full phone system, but all the questions might reduce the efficiency of evacuation. The partial system was deemed the best because a loudspeaker with a yes-or-no feedback signal could indicate whether the instructions had been understood or not. What impressed me most was that this creative experiment had been motivated not by theoretical inquiry but by practical necessity. This experiment illustrates so much about communication and feedback that it has become an exercise that communication workshops routinely use.

The other classic experiment that I was exposed to around this time was conducted by Hal Leavitt under Bavelas's guidance. Leavitt was a graduate student with Lewin and had just completed his seminal research on the effects of different group communication patterns on task performance. Five people sat in separate cubicles but could communicate with each other in writing. Slots between the cubicles could be closed, limiting who could communicate with whom. Each person had a set of marbles of all different colors, and the task was to identify the one colored marble common to all five people. The big question organizationally was whether letting everyone communicate with everyone else would be more or less efficient than channeling all the communication through one person.

Creativity in this experiment was the choice of task. When the marbles were simple primary colors, the hierarchical system and the fully connected system worked equally accurately, but the hierarchy went much faster. Everyone just shot their color data to the center person, who immediately figured out the answer and told everyone else. In fact, on repeated trials, the fully connected groups quickly developed their own simplified hierarchy. No wasted communication.

However, when the marbles were mottled and difficult to describe, the fully connected group solved the problem much faster and more accurately because they could develop a common language for describing the complex colors more easily than the hierarchy could. In the hierarchy, the group stayed too dependent on the leader; in the fully connected group, all the members encouraged each other's creativity, which enabled them to develop a new terminology for the mottled marbles.

The Bavelas and Leavitt experiments launched a series of communication studies with noteworthy outcomes. For example, my colleague Tom Allen later showed how the frequency of communication among engineers within a company was directly correlated to creativity and productivity, leading to important experiments in how to arrange physical space to maximize communication. Years later, when we tried to understand how Silicon Valley fostered so many creative enterprises, one important factor identified was much more cross-company communication among the engineers than was found in the East Coast companies around Boston.

I became aware that the field of group dynamics was flourishing and that much of the classic work of people like Festinger, Schachter, Thibaut, Back, and Deutsch was actually conducted in and around MIT. This was experimental social psychology at its very best, and I was smitten. Alex Bavelas became then and has remained one of my all-time heroes in the field. Had I had the opportunity in 1952, I would surely have gone to MIT then. But, alas, I was in the army and committed to at least three years of service as an army psychologist. Kurt Lewin and his theories stayed very much on my mind even though I hadn't met him. I would continue on as an experimental group dynamics researcher, and I resolved to pursue the Bavelas or Leavitt types of experiments in the future.

PhD (1952)

I finished my dissertation, which turned into a three-hundred-page document, half of which was a history of imitation theory. Allport was not only a stickler for good writing but also passionate about not forgetting history. It was a requirement that all his students' theses include a thorough historical analysis. I had all my data, and the analysis was fairly straightforward, so I only needed to do the history and write the whole thing coherently enough to pass the Allport writing test.

The hardest part of this was the actual production process. In 1952, we were still using typewriters and hired typists to put our drafts into final form. We dealt with carbon paper and ditto machines, which made blue stains everywhere. When we found an error, the typists had to retype a whole page, which often introduced new errors. Our relationships with our typists were crucial because they controlled not only the error rate but the length of time it took to finish something. It is difficult to describe how very different things were in the days before computers, spell-check programs, and fast printers. What could take months in 1952 can now be done in minutes while producing more attractive error-free copies. I was able to finish fairly quickly, get the thesis approved by Allport and Dick Solomon, and pass my orals. By the fall of 1952, I was ready to enter military service for real.

I could not have been more fortunate than to find that I had been assigned to a research unit back at the Walter Reed Army Institute of Research. I was now promoted to first lieutenant and went off to Washington once again to see what fate would bring. I did have to part with my beloved '37 Chevrolet, which had given me six good years of transcontinental travel and was still in remarkably good shape.

Chapter 6
The Walter Reed Army Institute of Research
(1952–56)

My years at Harvard broadened my academic outlook by exposing me to sociology, anthropology, and clinical psychology. The years at Walter Reed Army Institute of Research turned out to be even more broadening because of the kind of organization my new boss, the eminent psychiatrist David Rioch, had built. He had created a multidisciplinary group that consisted of several civilian and military psychiatrists, David Hamburg, F. Gentry Harris, and Doug Price; Joe Brady, an eminent Skinnerian behaviorist; several clinical psychologists, Sy Fisher, Hal Williams, Murray Sidman, and George Crampton; brilliant statistician Ardie Lubin; an ecologist; an endocrinologist; and several other experimental psychologists. Most were civilians, but we also had with us several enlisted men who had PhDs in psychology and who had engineered an assignment to this prestigious research group. Two of these, Win Hill and Sheldon White, became prominent professors after their military service. I've chosen to mention a number of them by name because they all became close friends; several were in my wedding and collectively became what today would be labeled a "high-performing team."

The group was full of creative energy and commitment to cross-disciplinary thinking. Rioch was a kindly leader who subtly imparted wisdom in his often-paradoxical remarks and questions, such as "If you want to find out about something, don't ask about it." I only realized much later the profound implications of that bit of advice. David's wife, Margaret, a prominent psychologist, influenced all of us through her presence at the many social events and dinners that the Riochs hosted. In later years, she became one of the proponents of the A. K. Rice Institute group dynamics workshops and ran these in the United States for many years.

I house-sat for them during one of their trips and found the experience quite intriguing and enlightening. There is something special about living in someone else's space for two weeks—the books, the arrangement of the furniture, the art on the walls, and all the little touches of how a home is put together create an aura that I found strangely stimulating.

This organization's mission, as articulated by Rioch, was to pursue research relevant to the army's broadly defined mission. Projects ranged from trying to understand shell shock or battle fatigue—what today would be called post-traumatic stress syndrome—to endocrine studies of stress and the effects of crowding in a colony. I was free to figure out how one could apply my interests in social influence to group processes and leadership. If someone had asked me to design a fun and productive postdoctoral experience, I could not have done any better.

Adjustment to life in the military did, however, pose some new challenges. I had to wear my uniform every day, learn to stand up straight, salute properly, and prepare to answer questions that might legitimately be asked of a first lieutenant in the Medical Service Corps on a military base. Most difficult was learning to show up at my office every day from eight to five and to keep my door open. My style up to then was to work at home at my own pace. I shared a nice apartment in Silver Spring with a fellow psychologist at the Walter Reed Army Institute of Research and would have much preferred to spend time reading or writing there, but army norms required daily presence and an open door if you were not talking privately to someone.

Much of my work was reading other people's work. If I was observed doing this in my office, nonresearchers walking by often asked me, "Not working today?" In a military environment, reading was not considered real work. Writing or meeting with people—that was real work. I certainly was not in graduate school anymore. I wonder whether in today's army I would work at my computer terminal and passersby would not know if I was reading, doing important writing, or communicating with others on social media.

Rioch believed in invigorating us with other points of view, so he regularly brought in academics like Erving Goffman, Fred Fiedler, and Leon Festinger to consult with us on our projects. Goffman was around a lot because at that time, he was studying socialization processes at St. Elizabeths Hospital, the big psychiatric facility in Washington—work that later was the basis for his concept of "total institutions" and his classic book, *Asylums*. Fiedler was doing his leadership studies, which showed that captains or coaches of basketball teams who saw big differences in their players' competence created more winning teams than ones who saw their players as more alike!

Festinger was developing his dissonance theory and writing about how doomsday cults react to predictions that do not come true. He predicted and confirmed that not only did they not give up their beliefs, but those beliefs actually became stronger after their predictions had been disconfirmed. Festinger loved to play chess with our statistician philosopher Ardie Lubin. Both were very good and alternated beating each other. We often wondered whether the main reason for Festinger's willingness to consult with our group was his desire to play chess with Ardie.

My love affair with Lewinian-type experiments, as illustrated so brilliantly by Alex Bavelas, led me to design a bunch of leadership studies that would be done with communication networks of the kind that Hal Leavitt had designed under Bavelas's tutelage. However, this work never led to much, primarily because of the distractions that were unexpectedly thrust upon me by virtue of being in the army, yet another kind of broadening as I reflect on these projects. The first of these distractions occurred just as I was getting settled into my Walter Reed routine in mid-1953.

Korea (1953)

The Korean conflict of 1950–53 resulted in a great number of prisoners of war on both sides. By the end of the war, about four thousand Americans and a few other UN troops were imprisoned in North Korea, and the United States had more than seventy thousand North Korean and Chinese prisoners in South Korean camps. As the conflict drew to a close, prisoner exchanges were negotiated, and it was decided to exchange sick and wounded POWs in April and May, what was called the "Little Switch." Though rumors had arisen early in the war that American POWs had "collaborated" with the enemy in the prison camps, these were not substantiated until the Little Switch repatriates came out with tales of forced indoctrination and collaboration. Pictures had surfaced of Americans participating in peace marches that gave the Chinese communists great propaganda photos to circulate to the world. On a more serious note, accusations had surfaced of American POWs "collaborating with the enemy" by informing on fellow POWs, signing peace petitions and in other ways "aiding the enemy."

On the propaganda front, another issue had surfaced. Thousands of our Chinese and North Korean POWs did not want to return home. To avoid being embarrassed by this, the Chinese announced that twenty-three American POWs also refused repatriation and would be welcome in China.

News from the Chinese mainland showed that the communists actively engaged in indoctrinating their civilian population through a "thought reform" program that emphasized "cleansing the mind of middle-class values" so that the communist ideology could be embraced. This involved intensive indoctrination, elicitation of confessions for various crimes as defined by communist ideology, and imprisonment based on the concept of prior guilt by virtue of class status. "Cleansing the mind" was translated by journalist Edward Hunter as "brainwashing," a concept that caught on immediately but continues to be misunderstood to this day, as we will see.[1]

---

[1] Edward Hunter, *Brain-washing in Red China: The Calculated Destruction of Men's Minds* (New York: Vanguard Press, 1951).

In any event, Americans' collaboration with the enemy was viewed as an unthinkable, historic first and led those of us in the services to wonder what we would find when the three to four thousand regular POWs were repatriated through Operation Big Switch in the late summer of 1953. The services then did something very clever. Since we did not know how many repatriates would exhibit signs of mental or emotional problems from the harsh conditions of imprisonment or, worse, from having been brainwashed, the army, navy, and air force developed a plan to diagnose and help where needed.

Instead of flying home, repatriates would travel by ship from Inchon, Korea, to San Francisco, where they would be reunited with family and friends. The sixteen-day voyage across the Pacific would provide time for mental health assessments and counseling and therapy, if needed. Implementing this program required pulling together all the psychiatrists, psychologists, and social workers available in the three services; assembling them into teams; and putting a team on each return ship. The teams did not get formalized until Operation Big Switch was announced and the repatriation logistics firmed up.

My participation, in typical military fashion, was launched by a telegram, saying, "Report to Travis Air Force Base within 48 hours of receipt of this order." That was all I knew at the time. At Travis, I met a lot of fellow psychologists, and it was then revealed for the first time what was being asked of us. We had to fly to Tokyo for a brief stay (the flight took much longer in those days because of refueling stops in Hawaii and Okinawa), fly to Inchon, report to our ship, and get on board and start the voyage home. Each team had a leader who was a psychiatrist (Harvey Strassman for mine), one or two psychologists, and one or two social workers. We were equipped to give tests and perform whatever counseling seemed appropriate.

This excited me, but I was also acutely aware that I had not received training for military duty in an overseas combat zone, which Korea still was. I learned that anyone who is to be sent overseas in this kind of situation must have a minimum of weapons training and a course of physical fitness. I had had neither. As is so often the case in the real world, even tightly structured bureaucracies with many rules remain ready to drop those rules when events demand it. Fortunately, war did not break out during my time overseas, so my incompetence in these areas was not discovered or tested.

Tokyo in 1953 was still a war-ravaged city—dark, lifeless, in ruins. We stayed at the local military hospital, tried to find interesting things to do during the day, managed a night club or two, visited geisha houses, and shopped for souvenirs at the local post exchange (PX) because little else was operating in the city at the time. The carved ivory chess set I bought remains with me to this day as a reminder of this trip. Unfortunately, the ivory pieces intended to be the black pieces, which were stained a dark brown, have faded to the point that black and white pieces are indistinguishable. I am now trying to cure this by bathing those faded pieces in strong tea.

Three Weeks in Inchon

We went on to Inchon and gained housing in military quarters on the big base that was receiving the repatriates. They arrived from the North Korean camps by the truckload, were processed, were assigned to quarters, and were to be moved to the ships within a day or two. We intended to make this logistically smooth so that no one would have to needlessly linger in Inchon.

When I arrived in Inchon, I discovered that these logistics had broken down and the ship I was assigned to was delayed for three weeks, so there I was in Inchon with nothing to do. I had heard about and read about the alleged collaboration and brainwashing, and we all knew about the Soviet communist techniques of confession extraction and indoctrination, so it was not a big leap for me to use this time to do a little research of my own. Suddenly, I had an opportunity to study a real case of social influence. I could see that the repatriates being processed had very little to do except wait for their ship, so I set up a little interview station, randomly pulled individual repatriates out at the end of the processing line, and asked them to tell me about their experiences.

I knew all about the problems of eliciting information in an area of social sensitivity from my PhD training, reinforced by Rioch's "If you really want to find out about something, don't ask about it." I took this to heart; I had to carefully avoid implying through any of my questions that I had an interest in how the communists had induced collaborative behavior. I learned to ask people straightforward, event-based questions, and I have continued to reinforce this learning style throughout my career. I introduced myself as Lieutenant Schein and said, "Try to think back to the day you were captured. Tell me what happened to you."

This pure form of humble inquiry allowed the repatriate to tell his story in his own way, with only occasional prompting in the form of the question "What happened next?" If someone stated something in general terms, I would ask for an example. If the repatriate said, "The Chinese soldier who captured me told me in bad English that I had been 'liberated' and would now be treated very well. That is what happened in the first day or so," I might then ask, "What would be an example of being treated well?" This prompt might elicit the response "Well, he gave me some food and water and was very nice to me as he took me to the prison camp." Repatriates differed in the degree to which they could tell their story, but the experiences of the POWs captured by the Chinese had remarkable similarities.

I learned that this so-called lenient policy of being kind to captives was carefully designed by the ideological leaders early in the Chinese communist movement and was part of their overall strategy in establishing the communist regime. Prisoners who were captured by North Korean soldiers told a very different tale of much harsher treatment and conditions of captivity. I also found right away that what the Chinese did had practically no overlap with what I knew of the Russian system of interrogation. Western analyses of the Russian methods emphasized ruthless, clever interrogators using Pavlovian conditioning methods.

Our unwillingness to believe that any American would collaborate with the enemy, even under such tough interrogation, led to wild speculation about the use of drugs, hypnosis, and other esoteric means of making the victim a willing pawn of the enemy. The movie *The Manchurian Candidate*, based on mind control through posthypnotic suggestions, cemented this image in the American mind. The

Cold War with Russia and our strong fear of communism made it easy to believe that the communists had unbeatable methods of mind control.

My interviews revealed that the Chinese used very different techniques in handling POWs, drawing more on their interpersonally sensitive culture with much more reliance on group forces and the manipulation of communication and the whole social milieu. The emphasis on extracting confessions had similarities in that during the growth of the communist movement in China, getting landlords and others who were considered exploiters of "the people" to confess their sins was viewed as an essential element of thought reform.

In the mainland prisons that we learned about later, new prisoners were usually put into group cells with prisoners who had already confessed and would, therefore, exert pressure on the newcomer because the cell's progress was evaluated collectively. In the POW camps, this same approach was used to manipulate prisoners who exhibited resistance and led others to resist. Such leaders were promptly removed or moved into isolation, a technique familiar to prison wardens in all cultures.

Everything reported in my interviews revealed a very sophisticated set of techniques for manipulating groups, filtering messages from the outside, and putting more pressure on those prisoners who showed some potential for malleability. In the prison camps, it seemed not to matter which prisoners signed a peace petition or participated in a peace march so long as a few provided the Chinese with propaganda material against the United Nations and the United States. In a large group, the captor could always find and focus on those individuals who were most vulnerable to influence.

Brainwashing Demystified as "Coercive Persuasion"

My three weeks of interviewing produced a fairly complete picture of what I later wrote in my paper "The Chinese Indoctrination Program for Prisoners of War." My two weeks on board ship involved giving tests to repatriates, further interviewing, and some counseling as needed. Most of the repatriates were immensely relieved to be out from under the physical and psychological pressures of imprisonment, and they welcomed the two-week trip home to decompress and recompose themselves for reentry into normal society back home.

The paper I wrote based on my interviews described in detail the prototypical experiences of an American captive of the Chinese. I sent this to the *Journal of Abnormal and Social Psychology*, which rejected it on the basis that it was too long. Rioch liked the paper and suggested that I should send it to the journal *Psychiatry*, which accepted it, and my paper became one of my most popular reprints. The testing on board the ship yielded a number of papers that I wrote with colleagues, one of whom, Margaret Singer, became a prominent expert on cults using indoctrination techniques quite similar to those of the Chinese communists. I evolved the term *coercive persuasion* and published a book by that title in 1961 to highlight the fact that if prevented from leaving, one becomes very susceptible to a wide variety of persuasive techniques that the captor may employ.

For my colleagues and me on the ship, and later back at Walter Reed, the repatriation provided an incredibly rich database that I mined for the next five years. Moreover, it fundamentally shaped my approach to data, to forms of analysis, to the selection of research problems, and to writing. I learned a great deal about research, about academia, and about how research data can become politicized and reveal fault lines in one's own culture.

Several examples stand out. On the way home, we gave everyone a personality test that revealed the embarrassing finding that the prisoners who had collaborated and the few prisoners who were deemed heroes because of their persistent efforts to escape had similar scores on a personality test scale that was labeled *psychopathic deviate*. It was a bit embarrassing to think of the heroic ones as psychopaths, but when we examined the individual items on which this scale was based, I then discovered that they all reflected a strong need to take action and weak impulse control. The researchers who developed this scale had identified this as the main characteristic of psychopaths, hence the name they gave the scale, forgetting that others in the population might also exhibit this temperament. It taught me to be very careful as a researcher in what labels you use to describe observed phenomena.

The second lesson taught me how the behavior of a few POWs was used politically to argue that the US moral fiber had weakened and that other POWs, such as the small contingent of Turkish prisoners, had shown much better resistance. My colleague Albert Biderman ended up writing a book, *March to Calumny* (1963), defending POW behavior and showing how the political attack on the US POW was full of misinformation. For example, several Turkish POWs were seen in the peace marches even though the Chinese had no Turkish interrogators and had little interest in converting any Turks to their communist beliefs.

I became personally involved as a result of a routine talk I gave to a management development program for US prison wardens in which I described the Chinese prison camp methods. In the mid-1970s, I received an angry, threatening letter from a group of prisoners in one of the US maximum-security prisons in Illinois. The letter accused me of handing the prison wardens a "loaded gun" with which to threaten and manipulate prisoners. I corresponded with this prisoner coalition and eventually cleared my name with them, pointing out that wardens were already very familiar with such techniques, so they found very little new in the Chinese methods.

The third example illustrated how rigid military policy can create unfortunate outcomes. Just before the twenty-three American POWs who had chosen to go to China were exchanged, two of them changed their mind and wanted to come home. One of these was a sergeant who was the leader of the group and had convinced the others to let him keep all the mail from home so that they would not feel tempted to change their minds. He kept all the mail and various US magazines in a locked trunk, but some days before the actual exchange, he looked at everything that had been sent. He discovered that much of what the Chinese had told him was not accurate and changed his mind about staying. He and one other POW came back only to discover that he was one of the people accused of collaboration, resulting in a court-martial and a sentence to many years in prison.

The twenty-one who went to China received dishonorable discharges. When almost all of them eventually came back to the United States, the collaborators among them could not be charged because they were no longer in the military. The leader who "saw the light" and saw through the communist propaganda, instead of being treated as a hero, spent many years in a military prison.

The main effect of the Korean repatriation experience was that it started to transform me from a dedicated experimental social psychologist to more of a clinician and sociologist, finding my research data in experienced reality rather than in contrived and controlled experiments. This experience had thrust me into a real case of social influence, and I found it engrossing.

Now for Something Different: Love and Tennis

Most of my colleagues at Walter Reed were married and had children. Being the only single one in the group, I could not escape the inevitable fix-up. In particular, one of my friends, George Crampton, made it his personal responsibility to see that I met suitable women. I had, of course, had my big romance at Stanford, a girlfriend at Harvard, and another one in my first year at Walter Reed. None of these had worked out, so I was pretty footloose in the 1953–54 period after my adventure in Korea.

I had also decided to be psychoanalyzed in Washington. During my three hours a week, my analyst dutifully sat taking notes behind me, hardly ever said anything, and was very interested in my dreams. One never knows how to evaluate such experiences, but suffice it to say that I felt then and continued to feel thereafter that I got very little out of it. Whatever deeper layers of conflict had manifested themselves as anxiety symptoms and had prompted me to get therapy briefly while a graduate student at Harvard have remained in my unconscious. I view myself in the category of "learning to live with my conflicts" rather than "resolving" them.

In any case, George Crampton and others were very much on the hunt to find a match for me. And their efforts paid off when George told me that this neat girl worked at the library and the information desk of the hospital. She was the daughter of an army radiologist assigned to Walter Reed, and, most important, a Stanford graduate. So I was marched over there one afternoon to meet Mary Lodmell, Stanford, '53, very pretty and single. George left us to talk; we enjoyed ourselves, and I remember being particularly struck by her spirit. When describing something that excited her, Mary kicked up her heels and did a little dance step. We made a date to meet again, and our love grew steadily over the next couple of years.

Courtship in the Washington area had its own special charm. Mary had acquired the job of administrative assistant to the director of the Advanced Management Program at George Washington University and had moved into a lovely apartment in Georgetown. I had moved into a fourth-floor walk-up on Thirtieth and M Streets that was incredibly hot in the summer but had a very bohemian feel that suited me perfectly. I was in a phase of trying my hand at abstract art with watercolors and acrylics, and I loved the image of being in this garret only four blocks from where Mary had her little apartment. I think we both reveled in the image of the romantic bachelor life in Georgetown, walking the beautiful tree-lined streets, full of large mansions and small-town houses, and meeting at funky restaurants for martinis and good food.

Mary and I both loved tennis. She, like I, had played on her school team in Carmel and had won the tournament as a frosh in high school, beating a boy in the finals. Playing singles with each other became a lifelong activity until her knees finally forced her to give it up in her early seventies. We developed what Mary called a "ballet"—I would aim my shots more or less at the center of the court while Mary tried to run me to the sides. That way, she got to hit her beautiful strokes while I got much-needed exercise. We rarely kept score because we were more interested in spending time together and making the ballet last with long rallies.

I found out that Walter Reed had a tennis team, which played matches against other military posts. I was able to join the team, become a regular in both singles and doubles, and bring back the wonderful tensions of competitive play that I had not experienced since high school. Mary attended all the matches and was, needless to say, my biggest fan. She had struck up a friendship at the hospital with Mitzi Streit, the daughter of the then post commander, General Streit. Mitzi married Roman Halla, who also loved tennis, and the four of us became close friends. Roman and I were very evenly matched, so we often had intense singles games while Mary and Mitzi cheered us each on and then joined us for postgame drinks, lively conversation, and dinner.

Life at Walter Reed suddenly became much more pleasant and balanced. I had survived the trauma of Inchon, I now had a ton of data to analyze and write about, and best of all, I was falling in love with a wonderful, intelligent, stimulating woman who had many of the same interests I had. Mary was willing and able to take my basic paper about the Chinese POW program and use her English skills to edit it into a manageable and readable paper. She was an army brat who, like I, had moved around a lot in her youth, had grown up mostly in San Francisco and Carmel, and, best of all, seemed also to be falling in love with me! In the meantime, I was still in the army and had to respond to the projects that the lab had assigned to it.

Testing Seasickness Drugs (1955)

In the winter of 1955, troops were regularly sent to Europe by ship on various rotational assignments. The troop ships carried several hundred men and some complete families across the stormy North Atlantic, which provided the services an opportunity to test ten drugs that were supposed to minimize seasickness, such as Dramamine, Marezine, and Bonine. We had to perform the test in a scientifically proper, double-blind way, so I was assigned to oversee the operation on three successive winter crossings. Presumably, my training as an experimental social psychologist and my availability rendered me fit to lead this project.

What did the task turn out to be? It taught me my first lesson in discovering the difference between an abstract set of goals and the concrete implementation of those goals. The plan was to give every soldier a pill as he went through the food line, get his name, make sure that he indeed took the pill, record where on the ship he was sleeping, and find out later whether or not he became seasick. The ten drugs and the placebo were randomly assigned so that we just drew pills in sequence from prearranged containers. I had one other officer and two enlisted men assigned to me to do the monitoring and recording. My job was to hand out the pills and supervise the overall execution of the project. As men reported being seasick during the voyage, we recorded where they had slept and later checked that against which drug they had taken.

All of this had been explained to me when I received a briefing on the assignment, but I then learned that to ensure proper motivation and to enlist the help of the troops, I would have to go before the entire contingent before we boarded ship, explain the research, and, in my commanding officer's role, *order* the troops to cooperate. I was advised that this was not the time to be a persuasive professor but to be a military commander. I received a warning that if I did not act sufficiently authoritative and convincing, the troops could subvert this valuable project in too many ways. I was reminded that the research carried sufficient importance to put an officer, me, in charge during the trip. We conveniently glossed over the reality that even under orders to cooperate, the troops had lots of ways of not taking the pills and thereby subverting the research.

Delivering those briefings, being properly authoritative, and being responsible for an important project involving hundreds of people initially seemed very scary. This was not me. I was the student experimenter relying on the authority of reason and logic. Being in command and giving orders along with explanations remained utterly foreign to me, but my superiors reminded me that I was an army officer and I had to do it. So I did it, found that I survived, and even enjoyed it, but my personality did not change much from the experience. I learned that one can do new things and one can rise to the occasion with new kinds of behavior, but those new behaviors do not necessarily take root and change the deeper levels of who we are.

The logistics of getting to New York, to the port, and on board the ship, where I shared a nice but small cabin and shower with another officer, were almost as difficult as the voyage itself, since I had a cold and was seasick for the early part of the trip. The troop ship also carried a number of families and spouses, so there were always movies, bridge, and some dancing. I remember practically nothing of this trip, but my letters home to Mary documented all of this in gory detail.

We got up at five to administer the morning pills for two hours and then again at lunch for two hours and at dinner for two hours, and then came some recreation and then bed. My men and I dutifully administered pills, made sure that they got taken, and recorded who got sick and when. We then turned the data over to statisticians back in Washington who turned up what proved to be quite interesting results.

The people who got the sickest were in the bow of the ship, regardless of what pills they had taken. The up-and-down motion, along with the yawing, proved to be very difficult to cope with, so even people who had received one of the drugs showed high rates of seasickness. Bonine won out over the other drugs, but even the placebo was more effective than not taking any pill. None of this was earthshaking, but I felt real satisfaction in contributing to practical knowledge and in managing the stresses of running the project.

After the long and basically boring trip, I found it exciting to land in Bremerhaven, where I stayed over for two days before reboarding the ship for the voyage home and more dispensing of pills. The most memorable part of this stopover was finding a local bar on the Bremerhaven docks and eating the best bratwurst and potatoes I ever had. After a week back in the United States, I was due to make a third and final trip, which made it possible to insert two weeks of vacation time in Europe prior to flying back home.

Oma Selma and Skiing in Europe

The two-week leave provided an unusual opportunity to visit my grandmother. The Iron Curtain was still drawn tight, but Oma Selma was a pensioner and, therefore, allowed to cross over into West Berlin at Checkpoint Charlie, where I could meet her. I presume they figured that if she defected, they would save some money. I took the train from Hamburg to Berlin, shutters drawn tight through the whole journey so that we could not see anything of East Germany, and landed at the tight little island that was West Berlin at that time. I then went to Checkpoint Charlie with Oma Selma's good friend Mrs. Schroeder and her daughter. Oma Selma was allowed to walk out of East Berlin to join us for a couple of days of talking, wandering around West Berlin, and eating many rich meals because food in East Germany was still marginal.

I had not seen Oma Selma since I was ten, and I found her to be a wonderfully lively, energetic little lady. Because Bad Schandau was a resort used by the East German communists and Oma Selma owned a nice house on the Elbe, which she turned into a pension, she suffered very little during the Cold War. World War II and the subsequent period of Soviet domination had been tough on East Germany because of severe food shortages, but Bad Schandau was so isolated and such a resort for the communists that it suffered no physical damage and was kept relatively well supplied. After a nice visit, Mrs. Schroeder, her daughter, and I delivered Oma Selma back to Checkpoint Charlie, where one could see past the gates into East Germany. How gray and run-down everything looked shocked me. West Berlin was still rebuilding and had many ruins, but color and vitality were all around.

It was now late March, but there would still be lots of snow in the Alps, so my basic plan was to go to Austria to ski. I had enjoyed skiing in Yosemite very much and had continued to ski in somewhat less pleasant conditions in New England, but I also remembered from childhood how much more spectacular the mountains of Europe were. I started in Kitzbuehel, Austria, a delightful village sporting many cafés where, after a day of skiing, one could relax, mingle, and ease oneself into pleasant dinners and evenings. What is in the United States more of a "bar scene" here consisted of "tea dances" with drinks of all sorts and, most important, pleasant music that smoothed the way for dancing and camaraderie.

The snow was melting in Kitzbuehel, so I decided to move on to the higher altitudes of Switzerland. On the train to St. Moritz, I met another American man on holiday, and the two of us had a truly memorable skiing experience. After two days of not-so-great skiing on the usual slopes, where again the snow was too soft, our instructor suggested that instead of doing the usual runs, we should go to the top of the mountain and take all day to gradually work our way down through the pristine powder snow. We would be the first and probably only ones doing this and would, therefore, have the experience of being alone on the mountain.

As predicted, it proved to be unforgettable. We would go a short distance and then stop to contemplate the grandeur of the mountains around us, beholding the large expanses of white above us with only our three tracks and the vast, untouched desert of snow below us. The silence of the mountain was striking once we got away from the hordes of skiers on the regular slopes. I found skiing in the deep powder very difficult and erratic, but this made no real difference because overall, it was so sensational to have it be just the three of us alone among the mountains. It did take us most of the day to work our way down, and we were quite exhausted by dinnertime, but it was worth it, and I continue to be grateful to this instructor for giving us this experience of a lifetime.

The search for good snow next took me to Zermatt, where I experienced both a wonderful time skiing in the shadow of the Matterhorn for a couple of days and a badly twisted foot on the third day. This ended the skiing and took me to Geneva a day early, where I realized while hobbling around the old city with a cane that the slower walking was a bit annoying but provided a much better sightseeing experience.

My leave then took me to Zurich and London, where I visited friends including Professor Edgar Meyer, my father's mentor after whom I was named, and psychologists whose work I had read in graduate school. I had written ahead, and I was pleased by how much these important professors welcomed me. I came home with wonderful memories, and I had sent home a variety of fun gifts acquired in the PXs at the European army bases, including a carved wooden chess set that began the foundation of a collection of chess sets that I treasured, along with my ivory chess set from Japan.

I flew home feeling that this army life was not too bad. I had written long and sometimes tortured letters to Mary detailing my adventures during this period but was very glad to be back and in my loved one's arms. The life of dating, tennis, and doing Georgetown resumed in earnest, but there was yet one more interesting army project to complete.

Studying Sleep Deprivation

It is fairly common knowledge today that in military situations, sleep and sleep deprivation are major issues, particularly in respect to guard duty and resistance to interrogation, but at that time, not very much was known about how people actually function if sleep deprived. So several of us were asked to conduct some studies with enlisted men who were assigned as research subjects. We set aside an area where the subjects would live for up to eighty hours without sleep. During this period, they would be tested at various times with a range of tasks. Some of these tasks required intense concentration and clear thought. All the men took the tests before the period of deprivation so that we had baselines for each of them. We then retested them after various lengths of time without sleep, carefully monitoring them to ensure that they had actually stayed awake.

The most striking result of the study was how well people could perform even after seventy-two hours without sleep. When called on to take a test, they could somehow pull themselves together and do almost as well as they had done at the beginning. However, they tired more quickly and needed longer recovery times between tests. As the number of hours without sleep increased, we also observed tendencies to drop into sleep spontaneously while standing or doing something active. To ensure that the subjects were actually sleepless for given amounts of time, we had to monitor them closely and jar them frequently to keep this walking sleep from happening.

As research administrators, several of us also experimented with not sleeping for longer and longer periods of time and confirmed for ourselves the remarkable ability of the human psyche to pull itself together when it gets challenged. I learned that sleeplessness is uncomfortable and becomes gradually more debilitating but that it is perfectly possible, for example, to be sleepless for a night, as when on an airplane going to Europe, and to still function perfectly well the next day in giving a speech or doing some consulting work.

What Next? (1956)

As the end of my military service loomed, the question of what next, both on the work and personal fronts, became more pressing. The courtship was going well, but it did not come without some stress on my part because I was ambivalent about commitment. I was very much in love and wildly jealous of several others whom Mary was seeing from time to time, but I could not bring myself to propose until early 1956 after two years of intense dating.

The hang-up was my learned caution—my tendency and preference to *react* opportunistically rather than to create my own situation. Though I do not recall it being a factor at the time, as I am writing now, I also suspect that uncertainty about my future career played a role in my indecisiveness. I knew I would be out of the army in mid-1956, but I did not know where I would find an academic job. However, this resolved itself in late 1955 with offers from Cornell and MIT.

Cornell offered a traditional assistant professorship in a good psychology department, and it would launch me as an experimental social psychologist. Ithaca was a difficult place to get in and out of but an attractive offer. What muddied the waters was an out-of-the-blue letter from Douglas McGregor, who was then a professor at the newly formed MIT Graduate School of Industrial Management. I knew the name because we had read some of his leadership articles in graduate school and I had attended one of Alex Bavelas's classes at MIT, but I really knew nothing about industrial management. The offer was to come to the newly created graduate school as an assistant professor and teach master's- and PhD-level courses in social psychology to management students.

In my job interview that spring, McGregor had made it clear that the school had adopted a strategy of teaching basic disciplines, such as economics and psychology, as an alternative to the more case-based Harvard Business School approach. I would be expected to continue my work in social psychology and explore how that would inform the practice of management. That part was attractive, but I knew that coming to an applied school would forever cut my ties with academic social psychology. In the end, the lure of working with Bavelas and the attraction of returning to Cambridge ("Charles River fever") made me accept the MIT offer, which meant beginning my academic career there in September 1956.

I did eventually propose that spring, and we held a big wedding at the Walter Reed chapel on July 28, 1956. It was a grand event that went off without a hitch, and I was a happy man. Mary and I decided to postpone our honeymoon until the following summer and concentrate instead on finding an apartment and getting settled into Cambridge before my teaching duties began in the fall. We sublet an apartment from Elaine Glazier, who had been a fellow graduate student at Harvard.

Our brief honeymoon consisted of a week of relaxing in Washington and preparing our cars and cats for the big move north and a new life together.

Chapter 7
Creative Opportunism:
A Reflective Epilogue

I've chosen to end this part of the story here because getting married, leaving the army, moving to Cambridge, and launching a new career simultaneously brought about a lot of changes that deserve a story of their own. I was now thoroughly Americanized and entering the next phase of life as a well-socialized young professor. What remains then is to reflect on what I learned during this first "learning journey." In the next book, *Doing It All*, the learning journey involves building a marriage, a family, and a career in Cambridge. Then in book three, I go into detail on what was involved in becoming a professor and learning to teach, do research, consult with organizations, and lead a small department.

To close this book, I need to reflect. Experiences without reflection do not provide much learning. The important learning comes from seeing oneself in action, considering the lessons in what one sees, and then looking forward with a new perspective.

What I see as I look back is something that I want to call *creative opportunism*. Let me first comment on the word *creative*. I once wrote an article called "Role Innovation" in which I pointed out that whatever job we have, how we do our work and how we play our role in our organization inherently involve creative components. No two people will perform a given job the same way. Instead of condemning this as *deviance*, or failure to conform to the rules, we should honor it as creativity. It should remind us that creativity is not primarily the province of the artist but a capacity we all have and use, or at least should use.

The common application of aesthetic terms to ordinary events and actions reveals the ingrained overlap and blurring of the pragmatic and the aesthetic. It is often quite appropriate to say that what we did was *beautiful* or *ugly*, and many life experiences can be assessed similarly. Doing things my own way was not always what was expected or what was *best* to do, but it allowed my creative side to express itself.

What of opportunism? In reflecting, I often find myself saying how *lucky* I was that certain opportunities were provided to me at various stages of life. The original title of these memoirs was *Right Time, Right Place*. Being placed at Walter Reed for my internship and, therefore, having army inductees available as experimental subjects who enabled me to gather all my data in the matter of a couple of months was certainly lucky. But maybe even more important is to recognize that my desire to make things work out for me is what led me to discover the induction center and to make the arrangements to use inductees as subjects for the experiment. That was creatively opportunistic.

Maybe a deeper lesson is to recognize how the combination of learned caution and careful assessment of new situations led to a skill in seeing and seizing opportunities as they presented themselves. Perceiving how their refugee status and successive moves from hostile environments traumatically impacted my parents, I learned to be cautious and self-protective but, at the same time, to utilize those very traits to help me and others. The fact that my parents had already established a link with the University of Chicago in the 1930s was certainly a necessary creative component of our evolved lives.

My decision to attend Harvard was a clear and deliberate choice to become more interdisciplinary. At Michigan, I would have gained training as a more traditional social psychologist and would have missed exposure to clinical psychology, sociology, and anthropology. Similarly, entering the Army Clinical Psychology Program was based not on luck but rather on a fear of being drafted. Those two decisions created the opportunities to come. Luck or good fortune is important in providing interesting opportunities. But what we do with those moments is our choice. My ability to seize opportunities was the result of repeatedly learning how to adapt to new situations and how to take advantage of situations that I had not brought about but could benefit from.

To put this succinctly, I can see in the content and timing of my past actions that they usually enabled me to accomplish something that I wanted or needed. No matter what was going on around me, I figured out how to use the experiences to my own benefit in the long run. Call this a kind of "reactive creativity." Either because I never learned how to create my own situation or because situations and relationships tended to be thrust upon me, I learned to be reactive, but not just reactive. Make something more out of it, and get good at it. Paradoxically, when I have a lot of free time, I seem less productive and less creative. When circumstances put me under pressure, my creative juices start to flow.

This attitude toward life is neither cynical nor idealistic. Rather, I believe it to be a kind of realism. Observe carefully, and then do what is most advantageous for long-range personal gain, but always do it with the knowledge that taking advantage of others—being selfish rather than self-protective—is not fully realistic. I want to compete, to win, and to get ahead, but I am careful not to hurt others in the process or gain an unfair advantage.

Fairness and justice have, therefore, developed as strong values in my adaptive style. If you don't want to be hurt by others, then don't hurt them, because it gives them license to retaliate. If you want to get ahead and be safe, do it through competence and by helping others, not by walking over them. The challenge of creative opportunism is to recognize the balance and flexibility inherent in it; one must always be attuned to both one's own and others' wants and needs, which often vary by situation and over time. Hence flexibility and agility are important skills to develop.

In summary, I realize now that if one has the adaptive capacity and some creative energy and ambition, one can play it safe and be timid in some aspects of life while being quite assertive and courageous in other areas in order to achieve ambitious life goals. Or, to put it another way, I found I could be simultaneously very humble and dependent when the situation was threatening but also very arrogant and self-confident that I would figure out a way to create something useful or learn something important.

A Final Thought on the Acculturation "Process"

I titled this book *Becoming American*. What does that actually mean, and what am I really trying to convey about the first three decades of my life? One clear conclusion is that once I learned English, life became progressively easier. Getting to Chicago, learning American culture, and finding out that I fit into it without much effort made life simpler. However, *becoming* American is not the same as *being* American. *Becoming* implies some experience of and insight into the *process* of shedding old cultural elements and acquiring new cultural elements. Living through several processes of learning new languages and cultural values provided sensitivity to interpersonal and social processes, which, I am sure, have helped and sometimes shaped the directions of my life and work.

On the other hand, undergoing such processes several times prevents knowledge of what it is like to be embedded from the outset. In later years, my wife, who was an army brat and who moved frequently during her youth, pointed out how easy it was for the two of us to move from one place to another, either as part of a travel itinerary or in connection with various sabbaticals. She saw us as rolling stones who gather no moss. The fact that I spent most of my academic career at MIT does not negate that point, because the difficult winter weather in New England caused us to travel a great deal and, once I was part-time, to even spend whole semesters away from Cambridge. We learned to live in many communities and many houses.

Another way to frame this issue is to realize that I am always at the periphery of things, mostly by choice. Such marginality gives one a broader perspective and the ability to see things that others who are more embedded do not see. Whether the inevitable bouts of loneliness are the product of this kind of marginality or the result of being an only child is hard to say. What I do know is that I often want to be with people, but the minute they want me to "commit,"

I find myself backpedaling and inventing excuses that allow me to return to my peripheral perch.

This leads to how the final concept for these memoirs came to be—"learning journeys." What marginality and frequently moving into new worlds have meant to me is that I truly enjoy the endless process of learning about people, groups, and organizations. The most fun I am having now at age eighty-eight is the new learning that I am getting from being a widower, living in a new locale, and building a new work life with new colleagues, friends, and clients. The most fun of all is watching my three kids, their families, and my seven grandchildren on their learning journeys.

Open Book Editions
A Berrett-Koehler Partner

Open Book Editions is a joint venture between Berrett-Koehler Publishers and Author Solutions, the market leader in self-publishing. There are many more aspiring authors who share Berrett-Koehler's mission than we can sustainably publish. To serve these authors, Open Book Editions offers a comprehensive self-publishing opportunity.

A Shared Mission

Open Book Editions welcomes authors who share the Berrett-Koehler mission—Creating a World That Works for All. We believe that to truly create a better world, action is needed at all levels—individual, organizational, and societal. At the individual level, our publications help people align their lives with their values and with their aspirations for a better world. At the organizational level, we promote progressive leadership and management practices, socially responsible approaches to business, and humane and effective organizations. At the societal level, we publish content that advances social and economic justice, shared prosperity, sustainability, and new solutions to national and global issues.

Open Book Editions represents a new way to further the BK mission and expand our community. We look forward to helping more authors challenge conventional thinking, introduce new ideas, and foster positive change.

For more information, see the Open Book Editions website:
http://www.iuniverse.com/Packages/OpenBookEditions.aspx

Join the BK Community! See exclusive author videos, join discussion groups, find out about upcoming events, read author blogs, and much more! http://bkcommunity.com/

Printed in the United States
By Bookmasters